ANIMAL RESCUE LEAGUE OF IOWA, INC.™

For Love of
DOGS

D1304245

Landauer Publishing, LLC

For Love of
DOGS

636.7
A598

This book was designed, produced,
and published by Landauer Publishing, LLC
3100 101st Street, Urbandale, IA 50322
www.landauercorp.com   515/287/2144   800/557-2144

President/Publisher: Jeramy Lanigan Landauer
Vice President of Sales and Administration: Kitty Jacobson
Editor: Jeri Simon
Contributing Editor: Carol McGarvey
Art Director: Laurel Albright
Photographer: Sue Voegtlin
Videographer: Tom Chaput

ISBN 13: 978-1-935726-12-8
ISBN 10:   1-935726-12-9

Library of Congress Control Number: 2011937121
This book printed on acid-free paper.
Printed in China

10-9-8-7-6-5-4-3-2-1

Table of Contents

Table of Contents

Table of Contents

ANIMAL RESCUE LEAGUE OF IOWA, INC.™

Founded in 1926, The Animal Rescue League of Iowa, Inc. (ARL) is Iowa's largest nonprofit animal shelter.

The ARL serves animals in need across the state, with a focus on Polk County and central Iowa. The mission of the ARL is to promote animal welfare, encourage and strengthen the human/animal bond and prevent the overpopulation of pets.

Annually, the ARL takes in about 20,000 animals from 61 Iowa counties and 9 states. Of the 20,000 animals, 9,709 were cats and kittens. On any given day, the shelter has more than 650 animals in its care at its main facility and four satellite locations. With such a large number of animals to care for and only 50 full-time staff members for five locations, the ARL relies heavily on volunteers to assist in all realms of the organization, from daily care of animals to helping with fundraising efforts. Currently, more than 1,700 volunteers donate thousands of hours of service.

The ARL is the only shelter in central Iowa that never turns away an animal in need. This results in a large number of animals and people who depend on the ARL each year. This dependence has grown dramatically since the ARL was founded more than 80 years ago.

—Tom Colvin, Executive Director
Animal Rescue League of Iowa

ARL-Iowa never turns away an animal in need.

The saying on the front desk, "Finding Your Best Friend • Share Your Love • Be A Friend", welcomes visitors.

Yvette guides families through the animal adoption process.

Indoor exercise and training center

In the Hug Room, adopters and animals meet and interact.

The puppy Roddick is in an adoption kennel waiting for his forever family.

Litters of puppies are kept together until adopted. Volunteers begin socializing and training the puppies while they are at the ARL.

ARL-Iowa's agility course inside Bailey's Bark Park.

The ARL-Iowa Rescue Ranch cares for abused and neglected horses taken from their owners by the court system until they are ready for adoption.

Spacious outdoor dog runs provide daily exercise areas.

The ARL-Animal House Retail Store offers specially selected equipment, supplies, toys and treats.

Photo by: Kelly Kesling,
Kesling Photography

Tom Colvin

Tom Colvin has been instrumental in the State of Iowa for animal protection work since 1974. He began his work on animal protection as a veterinary technician in Waterloo, Iowa. He went on to become the director of the Black Hawk Humane Society (now called Cedar Bend). Tom moved to Des Moines in January, 1993, to become the shelter director of the Animal Rescue League of Iowa, Inc. (ARL). In 1995, he was appointed the ARL's executive director, a position he still holds. Tom led the initiative to build a new 43,000-square-foot shelter, which was completed in October, 2008.

The Animal Rescue League is the largest animal shelter in the State of Iowa with four adoption locations and is responsible for the care of more than 20,000 animals each year, including a farm animal adoption program, and animal control for the City of Des Moines. Additionally, Tom started a prison program at Rockwell City Men's Prison, called Whinny, which provides extra care and rehabilitation for neglected horses that come to the ARL until they are ready for adoption.

Tom has also been the President of the Iowa Federation of Humane Societies since 1981, is on the Iowa State University External Stakeholders Advisory Group, served on the Iowa Board of Veterinary Medicine and the Board of the Iowa Wildlife Center. In addition, Tom was a wildlife rehabilitator and has served on Iowa deer task force committees. Tom has done extensive work on animal cruelty investigations and puppy mills.

He has worked tirelessly on legislation to strengthen Iowa's laws for animal protection. He has received awards for his efforts in legislation, including his work to enact the animal shelter mandatory spay/neuter law in 1992 and the felony animal abuse law in 2000. Recent successes in legislation have resulted in prohibiting giving pets as prizes, felony animal fighting laws, and in 2010, the passing of the Puppy Mill Bill.

Photo by: Kelly Kesling,
Kesling Photography

Paula Sunday

After being raised on a farm in eastern Iowa and receiving a BS in Zoology from Iowa State University in Ames, Iowa, there wasn't much doubt that Paula's career path would include animals, specifically dogs.

In 1980, after working as a Medical Technician with the Black Hawk Humane Society in Waterloo, Paula quickly realized she wanted to help owners solve issues that were causing them to turn in their pets—housetraining, play biting, chewing, digging, barking and other common dog behaviors.

By studying information from other trainers, attending national seminars, reading books and watching DVDs, she was able to use this information to help pet owners. Paula's goal is to teach owners to understand their dogs' needs and how dogs communicate. Thus, giving owners a chance to resolve problem behaviors through management, training and behavior modification.

She began working at the Animal Rescue League of Iowa (ARL) in the early 1990's. Paula evaluates shelter dogs to place them in the most compatible home. She also works with ARL volunteers on several programs to train and socialize shelter dogs and puppies before adoption. Paula responds to pet owners questions and does pet behavior spots on local TV and radio stations.

Her menagerie at home includes Tag (you will meet him in the book and DVD), Honeybear, a chow mix, cats Schwartz and Wink, 25 hens who were abandoned at the ARL, and a 33-year-old Appaloosa horse, named Cowboy.

Paula has been a long-term board member for the Iowa Federation of Humane Societies and a member of the Association of Pet Dog Trainers since 1997.

This book is the opportunity to reach many people with information that she hopes will enhance their relationship with their pets.

Photo by: Kelly Kesling,
Kesling Photography

Mick McAuliffe

Mick McAuliffe joined the ARL staff in November, 2009, as the Pet Behavior and Enrichment Manager. Before coming to the United States, Mick served as the Director of Animal Behavior and Training for the R.S.P.C.A. Queensland, Australia, where he developed assessment, modification and training programs for multiple species. In addition to his extensive work in canine training, Mick has applied his training skills to a variety of animals, from Sea World Australia's large marine mammals to serving as head avian keeper and trainer for a collection of 130 native and exotic birds and developing free-flight shows for visitors.

Mick has lectured on animal behavior across five continents, working extensively in Australia,

Japan, China, England, Saudi Arabia, and the United States. He believes pets live with us as part of our family, learning what we like and dislike through everyday experiences. He does not believe in dictatorships or set training sessions. Instead, he educates owners on how to teach pets our rules and guidelines each day. Whether you are sitting on your sofa or going for a walk, living is learning.

In Afghanistan, his experiences handling and training bomb-detecting dogs changed him forever. He says, "I wouldn't be here right now if it weren't for a couple of the dogs I worked with."

Training should be fun for you and your pet, not stressful. Mick trains using only positive reinforcement techniques, eliminating the need for physical or verbal correction or training equipment that can cause pain or injury. He educates owners on how to train their pets with patience and understanding, resulting in a well-mannered pet and a life-long bond.

Mick and his wife Caitlin share their home with four cats, their dog Lucy, and their birds Jack and Zane. All are rescues.

ARL
ANIMAL RESCUE LEAGUE OF IOWA, INC.

Current ARL Programs and Services

- Pet Adoptions at four Des Moines-area locations.

- Pet Behavior Counseling and Training classes (for dogs, cats and rabbits).

- Spay and Neuter Program (adopted pets spay/neutered prior to adoption).

- Spay the Mother Program (free spays to mothers of litters, free neuters to males).

- Humane Education.

- Lost & Found and ID Me Program.

- Pet Receiving (of strays and owner-released animals).

- Pet First Aid Training.

- Cruelty Intervention Program.

- Disaster Planning Service for Pets.

- Whinny Program in collaboration with Iowa prison systems.

- Volunteer Opportunities.

- Pets in Crisis (provide temporary housing for pets of people in crisis, i.e. house fire, domestic abuse, homelessness).

- Temporary Love and Care Program for special needs animals.

- Animal Assisted Therapy.

- Humane Euthanasia and Cremation Service.

- Legislation/Advocacy for animal welfare laws.

- Contractual relationship with several local government entities including the City of Des Moines to provide care and all Animal Control services to over 7,500 lost and homeless animals. These animals are found by the public or picked up or seized by the Animal Rescue League of Iowa Animal Control Officers, who provide the service for Des Moines.

- Horse Rescue and Adoption Program.

- Barn Buddy Program.

Current ARL Clubs and Services

Many times black cats seem to be overlooked in favor of lighter colored cats. There are different theories behind this, maybe it's because their facial expressions are harder to see, so there isn't an instant connection. No matter what the theory, the fact remains, black cats are the most commonly overlooked cats in shelters. Cats come in all sorts of sizes and colors and each has its own unique personality. It is this personality that draws us to them, not the color of their fur. Remember this the next time you are looking to add a new family member, take a good look at who is in that kennel, you might just find your new best friend.

Have you ever been to the shelter, walked down a line of kennels and seen mostly black dogs? Many times black dogs seem to be overlooked in favor of lighter colored dogs. There are different theories behind this, maybe it's because they are harder to see in the back of their kennel, so there isn't an instant connection. It is a dog's unique personality that draws us to him, not the color of his fur. Remember this the next time you are looking to adopt a new family member. Don't overlook the dog that could become your new best friend.

Pit bull terriers are perhaps the most misunderstood dog breed in the world. With proper training and responsible ownership, these dogs can be lifelong companions to people of all ages. The Animal Rescue League believes that a breed alone does not make a dog good or bad. It is our hope that through education, compassion and understanding, pit bull terriers will soon be respected for the amazing animals they truly are. Some have given them a bad reputation, now it is up to you to fix it.

The annual Raise Your Paw benefit auction is ARL's largest fundraiser of the year. A live and silent auction features hundreds of donated items and draws a huge crowd ready to bid. All proceeds are used to enrich the lives of the animals ARL is dedicated to helping.

The Pêt-à-Porter (pronounced pet-a-por-tay) Fashion Show is a spring ARL fundraiser featuring the latest in human and pet fashions. Pets ready for adoption serve as the pet fashion models and often find their forever homes with attendees of the event.

In 2010, the ARL opened a dog park called "Bailey's Bark Park", named after an ARL Alumni, Bailey. Bailey's Bark Park is primarily a place for dogs in adoption to be able to get out and run and play without the restrictions of a leash.

Make a lasting impact on the animals by becoming a part of the ARL's Loyal Friends Club! You can join the club by simply making a reoccurring, monthly donation of your choice to the Animal Rescue League of Iowa.

A Hands-On Journey

Of the many books with videos on dogs, to the best of our knowledge, this is the first developed by shelter staff based on 24 hours a day, every day experiences.

Our passion is caring for and about animals. We have seen it all—from purebred pups to designer dogs. From receiving wonderful, beloved dogs surrendered due to human life changes, to closing down puppy mills, rescuing pit bulls, to socializing pups. Animals are our life.

We are writing this book to help each of you who loves dogs select, understand, train and care for your dog, and to help you create the lasting and loving bond that will keep your companion in his home forever.

Tom, Paula, Mick

"A national leader"

"The Humane Society of the United States has partnered with the Animal Rescue League of Iowa, Inc. (ARL) for more than a decade on companion animal welfare initiatives. The ARL has proven itself a national leader in the animal sheltering field with innovative programs on pet adoption, shelter enrichment for animals, companion animal legislation, spay/neuter outreach and other initiatives that will better the lives of animals today and in the future. We are pleased to see the ARL publish a book that will help keep cats and dogs in their current homes while providing the enrichment they need to thrive."

Michael Markarian,
executive vice-president and
chief operating officer of
The Humane Society of the United States

"A state of the art facility"

"I was pleasantly surprised to find one of the best animal shelters I have ever encountered in an area considered to be the hinterlands by those of us who frequent the Washington-New York City corridor. The Animal Rescue League in Des Moines, Iowa, goes beyond being a state-of-the-art facility that pays special attention to the behavioral needs of the animal in its care. The cats in particular were happy, healthy, relaxed and had plenty of opportunities for interaction. The staff as well was tuned in to what it takes to help the creatures in their care find life-long loving homes."

Randall Lockwood, Ph.D., CAAB
Senior Vice President/Forensic Sciences and
Anti-Cruelty Projects
American Society for
Prevention of Cruelty to Animals

At ARL-Iowa, we never turn away an animal in need. We look at various options for dogs turned in.

We have behavior foster care, medical foster care and foster caregivers who take in litters until they are old enough for surgery and adoption. We screen dogs with potential for working jobs, such as drug detection, search and rescue and occasionally service dogs. We take every opportunity to save every dog that can be saved. Yet, with 50 to 100 animals arriving every day, tough decisions are unavoidable.

Some happy endings
from the Animal Rescue League of Iowa

Gone to a Good Home!

Photos by: Rachel Tabron
Ambroja Photography

www.ambrojaphotography.com
www.facebook.com/ambrojaphoto

Duke

Duke was a stray dog rescued from the Des Moines River in early 2011 by two amateur photographers. He had been shot, paralyzed, thrown into the river and left to fend for himself. The wonderful people at the Animal Rescue League of Iowa (ARL), along with the efforts of the Iowa State University Animal Hospital, saved Duke's life.

Handicappedpets.com donated a customized wheelchair to Duke, and he is now wheeling around like a pro in his forever home. Duke is gentle, loving, and very special. Many believe he is a Rhodesian Ridgeback mix. Some think he is a Mastiff mix.

$6500 reward has been donated to find the criminal that did this to Duke.

Overwhelmed by the outpouring of support, his new owner Susan Hollar wanted to share this to thank everyone for their kind words, donations, and love for a dog so many have never even met.

"Duke has joined my little family and I could not be more excited. I feel so lucky to be the one to show him what love is all about. The ARL has done a magnificent job with Duke! They have been there every step of the way with his rescue, constant care, and the important decision to bring him to the best - Iowa State University. Working with the kind people at the ARL and the ISU animal hospital has been an amazing experience!

My sincere thank you to all of those who have donated to the ARL in Duke's honor. While Duke is a strong survivor, he could not have done it without you. I am also so thankful for all of those who have followed his story, prayed for him, stayed positive and hoped for a happy ending. Or, should I say, a new beginning. I am honored to be the one to give him that.

So, his story doesn't end here - now he has his own Facebook page with pictures and updates. Please find him at Facebook.com/SweetDuke

Thank you again to all of the Duke lovers!"

Susan (& Duke)

Duke made his first public appearance since his adoption at the ARL's Raise Your Paw event in April 2011 and has raised over $2,500 for the Dog Walk & Fido Fest to help more animals just like him!

For more than 30 years, my professional career has been tied to dogs. Dogs that need homes, training, grooming, socialization, or veterinary care. Most of my time has been spent in animal shelters. From my first day at a shelter, it was clear that pet owners and adopters need help.

They need information from people who understand what they are going through. They need support to get through the stressful adjustment time after bringing their new pet home. They need answers to behavior questions. The tricky part is most people don't realize that the time they need the help is BEFORE bringing the pet home!

Paula

How We Can Help

In this special book, you'll find guidance and advice built upon a lifetime of working hands-on with dogs of all ages in many environments.

Last year alone, 20,000 animals came into the Animal Rescue League-Iowa. Among these animals were thousands of beautiful, wonderful, sweet, friendly, young, old, big, little, purebred and mutt dogs. The knowledge we have gained working with these dogs and their owners will make both your dog's and your life better.

Guidance and advice BEFORE you need it.

What Most Potential Adopters Want

Many people arrive at the shelter with some idea of the dog they want to adopt.

They think they want to train a puppy. They worry that older shelter dogs are ruined. They want a dog that's not too big, and that doesn't shed much. They want a healthy dog; a dog that's easy to housetrain and one that's good with children—all the time.

The reality is that with positive training both puppies and adult shelter dogs can be wonderful companions. Often, an adult shelter dog already has some training and could be the perfect dog for you. When thinking about children and dogs, health issues, size and care, ask shelter staff. They can help you make an informed and successful choice.

If housetraining a puppy is an issue, you can make the process easier by following the steps in chapter 7. or, to entirely avoid housetraining a puppy, adopt an older housetrained dog.

Other potential adopters fall for homeless, elderly, injured, or shy animals to save them. Often these matches work out wonderfully with TLC and coaching from a behavior expert. We have even made great advances with some "handicapped" pets, regardless of the handicap. Successful adopters call, mail notes or stop back at the shelter to show off their progress.

Other times, the challenges frustrate the Good Samaritan. After a month or two, the pet with special needs is brought back for the very reason he was adopted. We understand the fatigue, but it saddens us. The one good thing is that we now have a history for the pet which will help us find him a new home that lasts.

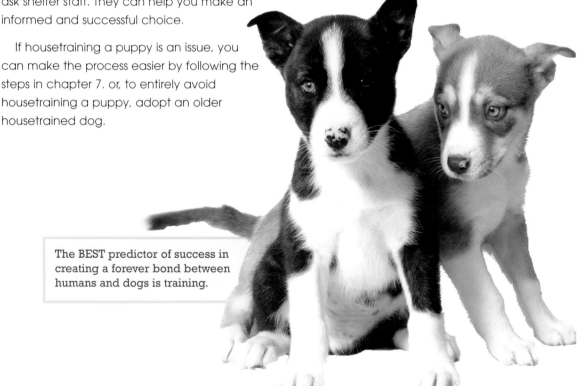

> The BEST predictor of success in creating a forever bond between humans and dogs is training.

Dog Tales

Charlie Bear, a young male German Shepherd, was picked up by an ARL Animal Control officer who immediately realized his forelimb had been severely injured. The ARL veterinarian examined Charlie Bear and throughout the examination, X-rays and tests, he demonstrated a great temperament, and spirit. The decision was made to amputate the injured leg, and Charlie Bear continued to show his great spirit throughout his recuperative period. His endearing personality was obvious to all and especially to the wonderful family that adopted him.

Creating the Bond

Throughout all our years of experience, we have learned that dogs stay in homes where there is a bond with the humans.

All other factors considered, if there is no bond, the dog will likely be gone someday, often with no regrets and even relief on the part of the human. Even if the kids are attached and the adults are not, the dog is at risk.

The bond can be attraction, love and/or training. Each one is able to keep the dog in his home but the best predictor of success is training.

So, how do you build a bond with a dog? Is it something chemical like falling in love?

Dog lovers all can recognize that instant attraction of "Oh my, who is that dog?" Sometimes it is love at first sight, sometimes it is just an inquiry into the breed or why it looks the way it does. What causes the connection? It can be our history with dogs or similarities to a dog we knew in the past. It can be a specific feature that catches our eye—big brown eyes, fuzzy ears, wagging tail or coat color. The package is the beginning and sometimes the end. People will disregard a wonderful dog because they don't like something in his looks. Often they discover their opinion changes dramatically after getting to know the dog.

The bond is also why giving a pet as a gift doesn't always work out. The ARL recommends gift certificates so adopters can choose their own pet.

Charlie Bear lost his foreleg yet, with his great spirit, found a wonderful family.

Creating the Bond *Continued*

What keeps a dog in a home for a lifetime?

Attraction and love can keep a dog in his home for a lifetime, but they are not enough. A dog needs manners. Unruly behaviors, unreliable housetraining, and even normal behaviors like digging, jumping and chewing can frustrate families. Frustration usually sets in after about six months. Owners realize they do not have time to housetrain, exercise and supervise a young puppy or dog. The children really don't have any interest in a pet that jumps on them or chews on their stuff. Eventually we don't like the dog we love. Even temporary frustrations can cause a total break in the bond. Often owners wait too long to help their pet when a little training, supervision, management and exercise could have taught good manners and kept the pet in his home.

The outcome is completely different when an owner realizes "Having a well-behaved dog begins with me!"

A Dog's Needs

Dogs are pretty straightforward creatures.

Their needs are simple and basic.

● **physical needs:**
play, food, exercise,
housing/shelter,
mental stimulation
to reduce stress
and excess energy

● **emotional needs:**
establish communication
and understanding

ARL-Iowa teaches only positive training techniques to create a lasting bond.

Creating the Bond *Continued*

Why is training the best predictor of success in creating a lasting bond?

We have learned that training affects the bond to the point where, excluding an owner's life changes, it is extremely rare for our shelter to take in a dog who has been through any formal dog training classes. The commitment to participate, the practice to get proficient, the peer pressure in the class to practice what you are taught, and the success people start to have at home with new behaviors really make a difference.

When people see a well-behaved dog, they regularly say "I wish my dog acted like that!" Often they have been able to train their dog or puppy to SIT but have become frustrated trying to train any other behaviors. After watching a dog who will SIT, LIE DOWN and do a trick on cue, owners are amazed and dismayed. They don't believe their dog could learn anything like that. Instead of crediting the training, they often assume the dog is a natural, was born knowing the English language or when watching the dog with a trainer, the dog's behaviors are somehow automatic. As a class instructor it is no small joy to show them how to help their dog begin to understand the behavior they want him to perform.

Birth to 16 weeks is an especially important learning time for puppies. Begin with gentle touch training. At ages 8-12 weeks, enroll puppy in classes that include basic manners and proper socialization.

Training starts early

Research shows that puppies learn very quickly during the first 13-16 weeks after birth. It is the right time to socialize a pup and start teaching manners and control. (See Chapter 3).

During this time, a puppy's brain is particularly responsive. It is the time when puppies should become accustomed to gentle touch and positive experiences. Humans should introduce the pup to the outside world by supervising the interactions of puppies with children and adults, and, by gently introducing the puppies to other pets and to multiple environments. From 8 -12 weeks is the ideal time to start puppy classes, a key element in bonding and training the manners needed to keep the puppy in his first home.

In contrast, when an owner doesn't know how or doesn't take the time to train the basics, a puppy can become a dog that jumps on people, chews inappropriately, gets into garbage, pulls on a leash, barks excessively or worse.

Knowing how important it is to train before fatigue sets in and before the bond is broken, we encourage owners to call us so we can do a short history on the issues and discuss options for their situation. (Refer to Chapter 10 for tips and techniques to correct Problem Behaviors.)

It is our goal to help owners communicate with their dogs through training and keep them in good homes for their lifetime. It is sad when the bond is broken and the animal needs to find a new home when good manners were just a few training sessions away. (See the "Nothing In Life Is Free" method of positive training in Chapter 8).

Be sure your puppy is current on his vaccinations before taking him to a puppy class.

As much as we wish all animals could stay in forever homes, we know shelters will always be needed.

While some animals are brought in as strays. Others are brought in when owners have major changes in their lives, such as illness, having to move to senior housing where pets are not allowed, or a work schedule that doesn't allow time for the pet, having allergies in the family, or being unable to afford a pet. Often for these families, giving up the pet is heartbreaking and traumatic. In these instances, a wonderful pet is now available for adoption.

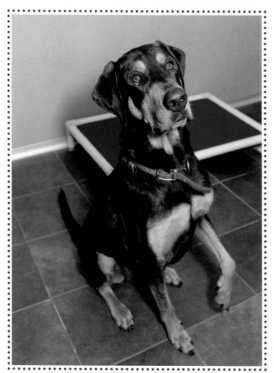

Communicating with your dog through training will create a bond that results in a lifelong home.

Fostering

When a pet is surrendered and needs an interim home to get him ready for adoption, the pet is placed in foster care. Volunteers foster pets for what are intended to be short periods of time. However there are risks in fostering. Part of the risk is falling in love with the pet. Then, there is the feeling of responsibility and fear that the right home won't or can't be found for him when he is ready for adoption.

There are no good or bad sides to fostering, but there are considerations to make before taking on a pet with special needs or a young litter that needs time to grow up. Bless those people who can foster and send them back to the shelter, grown up, healthy and nicely socialized. It takes a lot both physically and emotionally.

Paula says

Many people who foster tend to foster the breed with which they are most familiar or attracted to. When I decided to foster a Chow Chow puppy, even though it wasn't a breed I was familiar with, I felt pretty safe. I named her Fox and felt sure that after some handling and TLC, she would be able to go right into a new home with someone who understands Chows. I was right. Fox lived with us for 14 years and taught me alot about Chow behavior and communication.

Volunteers foster and socialize litters of puppies until they are ready for adoption.

Some happy endings
from the Animal Rescue League of Iowa

Dakota

Perry Police Officer Clay Leonard, a four-year veteran of the department, first met Dakota, a one-and-a-half year old German Shepherd, at Midwest K-9. It is a Des Moines company run by Polk County Narcotics Detective Dennis George, who takes and trains rescue dogs. The fact that George uses rescue dogs was a huge selling point to Officer Leonard and Perry Police Chief Dan Brickner.

George had six or seven dogs, all labs, available when Leonard first visited. After gauging Leonard's attitude and demeanor with the dogs, George decided to bring out Dakota. The two developed an immediate rapport.

Dakota is now Perry's newest K-9 officer. Dakota and Leonard, her handler, are certified in drug detection and will work together to help make Perry a drug-free community.

Dakota made a great first impression when she met the citizens she will be protecting. "Dakota was so good with the kids," Brickner said. "The dogs we had before were good, but I was always nervous about them with people. You can tell (Dakota) has got the drive necessary to be a good working dog, but she's also got the personality to be good with people."

The department plans to start a program with Perry's schools to bring Dakota to visit the students. The hope is that her bright eyes, lolling tongue and friendly demeanor will help deter children from becoming drug users.

"Dakota is a great asset...to have in our community to help keep drugs away from our kids and adults," Leonard said.

Dakota is a passive alert dog, as opposed to an aggressive alert dog. The difference is that aggressive alert dogs bite and scratch at the area when they catch the scent of a narcotic. Passive alert dogs will sit and stare at the location of the scent. Brickner said aggressive alert dogs can cause damage to property that the department would be liable for; plus, if the dog bites and ingests a dangerous drug, it could kill them.

All of Dakota's training deals with positive reinforcement. She is always rewarded for finding dope (a towel soaked in the scent of a particular narcotic) and those rewards will continue when she is on active duty in the form of a chew toy or tennis ball.

"They know what their reward is...and that's their ultimate goal," Leonard said.

Dogs are extremely sensitive to the tone of a person's voice, so just a stern command will be enough to get Dakota to pay attention. Leonard never yells at her or strikes her – or any dog.

Dakota lives to please. It is her greatest desire to earn praise from her handler and receive her reward for a job well done.

Story and photo by Laura Pieper, Managing Editor, The Perry Chief

Topics:

Dogs communicate through body language. From this timid-ears-back, whites-of-eyes-showing face (above) to a tail-wagging greeting (below)— every muscle is used to communicate.

Canine Communication

Watching dogs gives us the opportunity to identify their emotions such as fear, stress, anxiety, and love.

Misunderstanding how dogs communicate causes many handling errors for humans. We can make our dogs' lives happier and easier if we can begin to interpret their language.

Try This Quiz

- True or false - A wagging tail on a dog always means he is happy and friendly.

- True or false - A puppy with his mouth open showing his teeth is going to bite.

- True or false - An adult dog showing all her teeth is going to bite.

- True or false - Children always understand dogs can bite so children won't try to take their food or toys.

Hopefully you answered false to all the questions. We need to evaluate the whole picture of the dog, not just the tail, mouth, ears, or other individual parts. Dogs communicate with their whole body and every muscle has an assignment. We believe dogs want us to understand their communication, but since it is so different than our own, we do not always get it right.

There are major differences between human and canine communications.

Human communication is based on verbal language with some body language added for emphasis.

Humans make direct eye contact, often prolonged. We face each other in greeting, approaching in a straight line, holding out hands for a handshake, or hug.

Canine communication is based primarily on body language and uses very little vocalization.

Friendly approaches are head down slightly, tail wagging slowly from side to side and eyes to one side or the other but never with direct eye contact. It also includes sniffing genitals, noses and mouths for information about gender and who knows what else. That's only the beginning of the body language that goes on between two dogs. There are play bows, ear position, tail position, the face "frozen," mouth open or closed, body loose and wagging or stiff with hackles up. The dogs may meet on their toes trying to look bigger, or slink in, eyes averted and maybe even rolling on their back at first meeting.

Scent is a huge part of the greeting behavior. Even from a distance you can see a dog air-sniffing to catch a scent of a dog in the area. Sight can be important, but scent is the key followed by sight and then sound.

Dogs interpret information from other dogs through body language and facial expressions. Every muscle in a dog's face and head is used to communicate. The body language is measured in terms of millimeters of movement. A head turn to the right or left, lips tightened over the teeth, eyelids held still or tightened against the eye, even the muscles of the forehead and eyebrows make expressions other dogs can read and interpret.

Signs of a friendly meeting are when dogs approach each other at a curve, heads slightly down and eyes averted.

Refer to "The Other End of the Leash" by Patricia McConnell for an interesting look at how dogs interpret human behavior.

Dogs sniff the air to get the scent of other dogs in the area.

Licking may be a calming behavior.

A lab puppy in a play bow invites a reluctant older dog to play.

Calming and Other Signals

There are many signals dogs give us. Signals are often combined and may be conflicting if the dog is stressed, frightened or frustrated.

Dogs use every muscle, turn, weight shift, paw lift, eye movement and even their breathing rate to communicate. Since this a foreign language to us, we need to observe and identify so we can communicate with our own dogs. One reason we humans love having dogs around is because of the relationship we have with them. They "listen" and want to be near us. When you begin to "listen" to them, your relationship will become even more meaningful.

Licking

Licking happens so often we nearly always miss seeing it. Your dog may be using licking to talk to other dogs. It is very quick and often used in combination with other behaviors, like head turning. It can be a full nose lick or a flicking of the tongue just out of the mouth touching the lips.

Tail Wagging

Tail wagging is not a good singular signal of a dog's intent. A high tail wagging fast can mean the dog is highly aroused, intense, or agitated. A low tail wagging slowly can mean a dog is waiting to see what comes next. A still tail is always to be taken seriously, whether it is tucked under the body or standing straight out from the body. Movement is always better than stillness in the dog's language. No matter what the dog's tail is doing, take in the behavior of the whole dog.

Yawning

Yawning seems to be contagious, not only among humans but also among dogs. It acts as a stress reliever and should always be interpreted to mean something is concerning the dog. Yawning back at him can actually help him decide not to worry.

Turning Away/Turning of the Head

While it appears a dog turning away is accidental or even random, a dog turns his head for a reason. If he turns his head away from you when you are talking to him, maybe you are being unclear, stern, or a bit scary. Your dog may turn his head just a bit, or a complete 90 degrees. His goal is to calm you down and avoid conflict.

Observe when a stranger approaches your dog straight on. He will always turn his head to the side. The person is being a bit rude and your dog is being very polite. This is a great conflict avoidance behavior for dogs. They use it often and for many reasons. When you see your dog turn his head, try to determine why.

If you are petting your dog on one side, and he turns his head away from you, he may not enjoy the petting. Try changing where you are petting him and see if he turns toward you.

Yawning acts as a stress reliever.

When a dog turns his head away from you while petting, try petting a different place on his body and see if he relaxes.

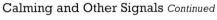

Pip is ready to play and Elle is turning her head to say, "Not now."

Calming and Other Signals *Continued*

Play Bow

Play bow is an invitation to play signal. Dogs use it with humans, other dogs, and even other species. You will notice the lowered front legs as the dog hops from side to side.

Dogs also use play bow to avoid conflict and to calm fearful or nervous dogs. If you watch a group of dogs and a new dog approaches, the group usually stands still until a dog in the group does a play bow. Everyone calms down and often there is a play/chase session. Sometimes the dogs just calmly walk away.

Sniffing the Ground

Sniffing the ground is a signal that seems random until you start observing how purposefully dogs use it. Dogs do sniff a lot, because they want to know what dogs have been through the neighborhood. If your dog is approached by a person or another dog he may lower his head to sniff, indicating he is no threat, and his effort is to avoid any conflict or confrontation.

Walking Slowly

Walking slowly is an interesting behavior to watch in a group of dogs. Sometimes when the play gets too rough, loud or a new dog approaches, all dogs slow down into what appears to be slow motion. Sometimes you will see a young dog ignore the others and just slam around into the other dogs. He will probably get a growl, snap or other correction from one of the adult dogs. This will help him to concentrate and see what the others are doing. Dogs are great at learning to mimic other dogs, so chances are he will quickly slow down. Speed can be too arousing and confrontational.

Watch your dog as he approaches something novel, like a toad. Chances are he will slow down and approach softly, evaluating whether it is a toy, food or something dangerous.

Sniffing the ground may seem random, but dogs use this action to avoid conflict or confrontation.

We can use this moving slowly behavior with fearful or shy dogs. In combination with several other behaviors it can help a shy or anxious dog calm down and be more interactive. Other behaviors to use with especially shy or undersocialized dogs are turning away, yawning, avoiding direct eye contact, and getting down to their level so you are not leaning over them.

Watch your own dog when you call him. If he is slow in responding, take a look at your body language as well as his. Does he start out quickly and then slow down, turn his head or stop to sniff the ground? This can look like he is ignoring you on purpose and it can be very frustrating. Can you help him come more quickly by turning your head or body to the side, yawning, using a softer, friendlier tone of voice or moving slowly away from him?

Freezing

Freezing is when a dog stops all motion and is totally still, usually only for a split second. Dogs use it to communicate a warning. If a dog has a bone or something else valuable and he freezes as you approach, he is trying to get you to go away. He will also use this with other dogs and pets in the household. Of course, children don't understand why the dog freezes. If the child continues to approach after a dog has signaled concern by freezing, he may start to escalate his communication to the obvious but unacceptable growl, snap, bite behavior.

Fearful dogs use freezing behaviors to try to relieve conflict. It is often used in combination with other behaviors, such as slow motion, depending on the dog's communication efforts. It is an important behavior for humans to understand.

Pawing

Some dogs paw to try to get a person's attention. It as a behavior that is also used to appease a conflict if the human seems distressed or angry. We rarely see pawing used with other dogs, just with humans.

Calming and Other Signals *Continued*

Rowdy Puppies

You will sometimes see an adult dog sit down with rowdy or playful puppies. They try sitting down to calm them. If that doesn't help, they may turn their back or turn and stare or freeze, gradually escalating their behavior to try to calm down the puppy. If the puppy doesn't recognize and adapt to these communications there can easily be a fight between the two dogs.

1. Fourteen-year-old Sadie sits to calm the rowdy puppy Bella.

2. Bella is ready to pounce. Sadie turns her back.

3. Bella's rowdy behavior escalates. Sadie tells Bella to "cut it out."

4. All's well.

Walking in a Curve

We often force our dogs to walk straight toward each other on sidewalks or in other circumstances. For the dog this is a very rude and confrontational behavior. This could be one reason so many owners have barking and lunging dogs when they are out for walks. It will help a dog if the owner allows even a small curve, whether it is on the sidewalk, going across the street, into the grass or a driveway. The more anxious or concerned your dog, the bigger the curve should be.

Smiling

Smiling occurs when the front of a dog's face contracts up and down to show the teeth. The dog may also draw his lips back to show all his teeth. The difference between this behavior and a dog that shows his teeth in a snarl is the rest of his body language. A snarling dog is stiff or crouched, his eyes dilated and he is scary overall. A smiling dog's body is relaxed while it is lowered and with a low tail wag. Eyes will be soft and slightly squinted.

Dogs do smile.

Submissive Urination

We often get calls about submissive urination from frustrated owners who believe this is a housetraining problem. It is very different, because the dog or puppy that rolls on his back or squats and urinates is being very respectful and as subordinate as he knows how to be. If this behavior is done to another dog, the dog is satisfied and walks away. If we can learn to predict the behavior and change our approach to the dog, we can often teach a dog he does not need to be this submissive with us.

Avoid eye contact with the dog and approach him from the side instead of the front when coming home. Greet your dog from a bended knee position so you look less intimadating or threatening to him. Refrain from scolding him for urinating, as this will only make matters worse. See the story on page 38.

Flirting

Flirting is acting silly like a puppy, jumping in the air, grabbing a toy to shake or toss, and just running in circles acting amusing. By getting us to laugh, or getting the dog to play, he has diffused all confrontations and conflicts, which was his goal.

Observing Your Dog's Signals

Dogs want us to understand them and may exaggerate their behaviors in an effort to help us. They will exaggerate their behavior with other dogs, especially puppies to give them a chance to understand them.

Dogs with little social interest, experience or attraction to humans make no effort to make their behavior known. Often dogs who are this subtle have been considered dangerous dogs who growl, attack or bite "for no reason at all" because their signals are too subtle for humans to notice or understand. These dogs often end up in shelters labeled aggressive by their owners.

Observe your dog's signals in your home when you need to move him out of your way, or he has his toys, bones or food bowl. If you scold your dog for some infraction, watch his behavior. That look is not guilt. Rather, those behaviors are appeasement behaviors with intentions of calming you down, not admitting to being "bad." Observing your dog's calming signals can be helpful on walks, at the veterinarian's clinic, and any time your dog meets new people, dogs, or children.

Dogs Interacting with Dogs

Puppies playing is a great time to start observing signals. Whether it is a litter of siblings or a play group from a class, you may notice every 15-20 seconds everyone stops for a few seconds. This isn't really a "freeze", but stillness, and then they will start playing again. Watching these puppies allows you to see many behaviors, including sniffing, freezing, lip and nose licking, and play bowing.

Dog Communication: A Visit to a Dog Park

When a new dog comes into an area, if dogs are allowed to do their normal greeting and sniffing behaviors, usually everyone gets along fine.

Adult dogs will often stop play for a few seconds, too, especially if a new dog comes into the group. Watch dogs at a dog park, especially if there is a group and a new dog comes in to play. The group will surround the new dog, sniffing him for a bit, then everyone will take a break for a few seconds. Suddenly one dog will do a play bow and everyone is off and running. Most dogs do not want a confrontation, and if allowed to do their normal greeting behaviors, will get along just fine.

Dogs on a Leash

Trouble can come when the dogs meet on leash. Owners concerned about how their dog will behave may crank the leash tightly and bring the dog close to them. This will change the body language and communication between the two dogs. Pulling on the leash makes the dog strain against the collar, giving him the appearance of being aroused, intense and possibly unfriendly. Allowing a loose leash gives a dog the freedom to give appropriate body language and prevent problems. Allowing the dogs to approach in a curve, sniff the ground, keeping things calm will make the meeting smoother and friendlier.

Also, while we want our dogs to be social and polite in public, they do not need to meet and interact with every dog along the way. Walking nicely beside you and ignoring the other dog is fine.

A dog on a tightly-held leash may appear to be unfriendly to an oncoming dog.

Teach your dog to walk on a loose leash.

Dog Tales

I adopted Fox, my Chow Chow, from the ARL at the age of about four months. She came into the shelter at about nine weeks old by a nice lady who had bought her from a breeder. She was assured by the breeder that Chows are great with kids, and they look like little teddy bears, so after she brought Fox home, she let the kids take her out to play. I have no idea how much socialization Fox had before she was brought into her new home, but she was very frightened and learned quickly if she struggled, growled, and snapped, the kids would leave her alone. The lady called the breeder back explaining how aggressive the puppy was.

She could return the puppy but no refund, and she really felt the man would just sell her again and put another family through the grief of having to give up a puppy that was terrified of kids. So she turned her into the ARL, hoping someone could adopt her with no small children and she would be okay.

Fox eventually learned not to be so afraid of children, even though I occasionally had parents recognize her breed and quickly lead the children away. Fox decided she would lie down slowly and let children scratch her tummy, which kept children from being in her face and everyone had a good time.

When Fox met children in public spots, where I couldn't let her decide to roll on her back, I gently held her head and guided the child to her furry back and even her tail. She just really didn't want children staring into her big brown eyes or examining her dark blue tongue. (Chow Chows have blue shaded tongues.)

Observing Your Dog's Signals *Continued*

Dogs Interacting with Children

Children are vulnerable because they approach dogs as if they are other children. They want to hug the dog, look in his eyes and ears, pick up his paws and catch his tail. In canine language this is a young animal with very poor manners and many dogs try to show their displeasure in very simple ways. Often the first signal of concern is a dog freezing when a child tries to hug him. Everyone thinks the dog loves the interaction because he doesn't move away. The adults may assume the children can hug the dog any time and will not notice any concern from the dog until he actually growls, lifts his lip in a snarl, or snaps at the child. Adults need to supervise a child meeting a dog.

Watch for signals such as head turning, lip and nose licking, yawning and freezing. Help the dog out if he is showing concern. Hand the child a toy or start a game with the dog. By doing this you have changed the dog's concern and hopefully relieved his anxiety. You may also ask the child to leave the dog and do something else.

Teach your child how to behave properly around dogs.

Observing Your Dog's Signals *Continued*

Ideally, here is what you might see when a child and dog interact and the dog is enjoying the relationship.

- When the child approaches the dog, the whole body of the dog is included in the wagging tail. You see a dog whose whole body has become a wiggle.

- The dog's eyes are squinty, slightly closed and blinking, his ears are soft and floppy or laid softly against his neck, and the tail is level or below the height of his body and wagging smoothly side to side or possibly in a circle.

- He should be flexible, not frozen and should approach the child as the child approaches him, unless restrained by the owner. Many dogs will be close to eye level with toddlers and do not attempt to jump on them because they can greet them face to face. The dog may check hands for food, shoes to see where the child has been and sniff faces and mouths to see what they have been eating.

- If the child is familiar to the dog and they usually play or cuddle, the dog may lie down to show his belly for a tummy scratch. We have seen dogs learn to control children by offering their belly to rub rather than trying to scare them away or threaten them.

Ask permission before allowing your child to pet an unfamiliar dog

Adults always need to supervise a child meeting a dog.

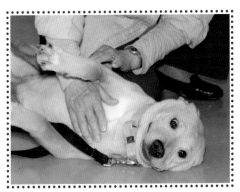

Some dogs enjoy a belly-rub.

Ears back, turned head, tail down

Tight mouth, big eyes, dilated pupils

Refer to "On Talking Terms with Dogs: Calming Signals" by Turid Rugaas to learn how to recognize your dogs communication signals.

Observing Your Dog's Signals *Continued*

Dog's Warning Signals

- The dog hurries to hide behind you.

- The dog shuts his mouth tightly.

- The dog's tail stops wagging or he tucks it up under his belly.

- The dog's ears lay flat against the back of his head.

- The hair on the dog's back from his shoulders to his tail starts to stand up. Sometimes it is the whole length of his back, sometimes just the shoulders and hips.

- The dog's eyes get big, he doesn't blink and his pupils dilate, making his whole eye look black.

- The dog vocalizes, whether a whine or a bark.

Any or all of these signals show distress, fear and alarm. Step in front of your dog, and stop the child from approaching and see if your dog can calm down. If he is still retreating, tell the child your dog doesn't feel well and doesn't want to meet someone and walk your dog away. Then you will want to work with your dog on helping him be happier and calmer around children.

If your dog sees a child approaching and his tail goes very high over his back, his body position goes forward, ears forward and he is up on his toes, we would be concerned your dog is threatening to the child and should be walked away. Some dogs just want to play but can be too rough for small children. Allow the child to approach only when the dog is in a sit position and the child can pet his back or sides. The front paws of a large dog could scratch or injure a small child.

Observing Your Dog's Signals *Continued*

We always encourage owners to be a bit assertive with other people, especially children approaching your dog. Even if your dog normally loves children, if you interpret his body language to say he is concerned, then help him out by asking the children approaching to stand still for a moment. Then, using treats and your voice, praise your dog, steady his head and allow the children one by one to pet his side or back in a gentle way. Each situation can be different for your dog, and we often don't see or understand if there are other stressful things going on around him.

Treat and praise your dog when allowing a child to pet his side or back.

Watch the Face

Caller: *My dog wags his tail and seems friendly to strange dogs when we are out walking, but when they get close to him he growls, barks and lunges. Why does he act friendly if he isn't?*

Paula says: *When a dog is put in a situation where he is uncomfortable, he has limited ways to communicate his concerns to us. Many dogs are not comfortable with face-to-face meetings with strange dogs and will give subtle but clear signs to his owner and the other dog. When those signs are ignored, he must escalate his communication to make it perfectly clear he doesn't want this meeting to happen.*

Watch your dog's face and body language. Are his eyes wide open in alarm or slanted and squinty in friendliness? Is his mouth tight, lip tight to his teeth, lines showing below his eyes or on his forehead in concern? Or is he panting, mouth open, face, and ears relaxed in greeting? Is he up on his toes, hair along his spine standing on end, stiffened in alarm? Or is he loose in his body, sitting or hanging out, relaxed and ready for a play date? The more we learn to read our canine's body language, the more he can rely on us to help him in new situations.

Submissive/Excitement Urination

Caller: *Why does my dog Sadie urinate in front of me when I come home? She is usually housetrained, but when I get home, instead of going outdoors, she proceeds to urinate all over the floor. When I scold her, she rolls on her back, sometimes even in the urine. Then she needs a bath, which she hates.*

Paula says: *Sadie, who is a young female mix, is so excited to see her owner, Mike, when he gets home, and initially his greeting to her was filled with excitement and fun, too. What has probably happened is that Sadie became so excited she urinated, which started a "trickle down" series of events to make her excitement urination worse.*

Mike, thinking she is urinating in the house on purpose, maybe to punish him for being gone so long, starts to scold Sadie. Startled and concerned, Sadie resorts to dog language for, "Please calm down. I am being as submissive as I can, including showing my vulnerable belly and urinating to please you." Mike is mad at Sadie and Sadie, trying her best to be submissive, frustrates Mike even more. Soon, each time Mike looks at Sadie, she squats and urinates.

To greet Sadie, I suggest Mike enter the house silently, not looking at or speaking to Sadie. Take her right outdoors to potty and greet her there, but practice a calm greeting. Also, Mike might want to practice some dog behaviors that can help Sadie be calmer and more in control.

Instead of facing her straight on, turn 90 degrees to the side, and bend your knees or squat down. If she is still nervous, try yawning, big enough so she notices, but don't pull your lips back. Keep your teeth covered so you look less threatening. Don't try to make direct eye contact. Let Sadie come to you; keep your hand low with the palm down. If she starts to squat from excitement, turn away to take the social pressure off her, and let her approach again.

Practicing this outdoors makes it easier for Mike, so if Sadie does urinate, he isn't upset. A few days of low-key greetings using dog behavior that is calming and appropriate and most dogs can start to handle greetings that get a bit more exciting.

Some happy endings
from the Animal Rescue League of Iowa

Ben

Ben came into the ARL thin, matted, unneutered, with gums that had grown over many of his teeth, several growths and heart problems. He was thought to be about 8-years-old and could not be put up for adoption due to his medical issues. It was estimated by the ARL medical staff that Ben would not live more than 6 months. At the time, I was working at the ARL and my family took him in as a hospice case.

Why did we take him in? We fell for his looks and were impressed with his unique size and appearance. In addition, he was the sweetest, most gentle dog and I felt sad that he had never lived a good life. I spent a few hours giving him a bath and cutting off his matted hair; he seemed so grateful and charming. We had the space, time and money, as well as access to vet care at the shelter, there wasn't any reason not to offer him hospice care for a short time.

The first day we brought Ben home, he jumped on the counters, peed/pooped in the house, climbed onto the sofa and stole food off the counters. He was too big for the largest crate and he never slept through the night. If we didn't get him outside quickly enough, he would potty on the wood floor in the hall. It was like a small pond. The pooping wasn't any better because he nearly always walked through it. I had to clean up where he had tracked AND dig it out of his giant paws. We had to start paying the pet sitters more because we knew he would wake them up multiple times and go potty in the house.

One night he became very ill and I called Dr. C and met him at the ARL. By the time I got there, Ben couldn't get up and his gums were totally gray. We talked about putting him down, but when Doc came back I decided I would just take Ben home and let nature take its course. My daughter and I slept next to him on the family room floor that night and in the morning Ben was looking at us totally fine. That was less than a year into having him.

Despite all his issues and stubbornness, Ben was the kindest dog I have ever known. He never showed one ounce of aggression. He volunteered at the Clive Library where the children were invited to read to a dog, no adults allowed. He was just a big, fluffy pillow. The way he moved made people laugh and smile. The way he looked into my eyes made me melt.

When Ben had had several instances of needing help to get up, we called Doc and asked him to come help Ben one last time. By then, I no longer worked for the League, so it meant alot that he came out to the house. We went into the yard and let our big friend go on a beautiful, Iowa afternoon. It crushed us and we were relieved all at the same time.

Would we do it again? I dream of having another Wolfhound some day, but the timing needs to be right. Part of why it worked was because I worked for the shelter. Honestly, the number of medical issues Ben had and the costs that would have been involved in treating him would have been quite high, especially since we also had two dogs, a cat and two rats at the same time, as well as a child in college. Having an Irish Wolfhound with no house manners and medical issues was a lot to tackle. Having Doc and being able to bring Ben to work at the ARL made it very doable. We love the breed and would love to have another one; yes, we would probably do it again.

Maryann, Steve and Kayla

Gone to a Good Home!

developmental stages and socialization opportunities

Developmental Stages and Socialization Opportunities

Most of the information on raising, socializing, and training dogs starts after puppies are eight weeks or older— the age puppies are available from a breeder, pet store, friend, newspaper ad or shelter.

Much of a dog's personality, temperament and abilities are developed during those first eight weeks.

Genetics and the mother dog have a great effect on the kind of pet your puppy will become. Try to see her during those early weeks and learn about her social, physical, and mental health. You want to be sure she is healthy in all these areas. A good time to meet the mom and pick a puppy from the litter is when the pups are four to six weeks old. Before then, the mother may be very protective and wary of strangers. This should be easy to do if purchasing a puppy from a breeder, but may not be possible when adopting from a shelter. However, you will want to ask about the mother to find out if she was friendly in the foster home.

Mia came into ARL as a very pregnant stray. She gave birth to a litter of 8. After a thorough health check, removal of dozens of ticks and a good bath, she was placed in foster care where she's taking very good care of her pups. Mia's great disposition has endeared her to all who meet her.

The following are general guidelines to help you understand the stages in development, early socialization, and training.

Gestation

Gestation lasts approximately 62 days. During this time, the mother should be well cared for in a safe, warm, comfortable whelping pen so she whelps her puppies without incident. She should be eating quality, high protein food and visiting the veterinarian.

Birth to Twelve Days

Puppies are blind and deaf from birth to approximately twelve days old. Their sense of smell is good enough to find mom and nourishment and to start to learn about their environment through scent and touch. They need to be briefly handled each day and checked to be sure they are gaining weight. At twelve days old, puppies begin to see and hear.

Thirteen to Twenty Days

From thirteen to approximately twenty days, the puppies mostly eat, sleep, grow fast, and explore their environment. At this age, they should start to spend more time with people and be handled individually. A few minutes of handling each day will make a huge difference in the puppy's future comfort level with humans. Each foot, nose, and ear should be gently touched. Puppies begin to recognize people's voices and scents. They will begin to play with each other and each puppy is starting to show some personality and preferences.

Puppies should be protected from extreme cold and heat and very loud noises.

Pups are blind and deaf at birth until they are about 12 days old, but are able to smell from birth.

Three Weeks (21 Days) to Seven Weeks

From twenty-one to forty-nine days, puppies change fast. They will gain coordination and their senses are developing rapidly. They should be introduced to handling by many people, especially supervised children, meet gentle adult dogs, and get lots of individual attention. Any puppies that show fear or anxiety should get some extra handling and attention to help prevent behavior problems later in their lives.

Puppy weights need to be monitored to be sure no puppy is being prevented from its share of the nursing or food. At three to four weeks, ground and soaked dog food (gruel) can be offered. When offering the puppies food, the mom should be separated for a few minutes. The puppies may sniff and lick the food, but depending on their supply of mother's milk, they may not be interested in eating the first few days. Usually by four weeks, they are eager to supplement milk with gruel and dig in.

Puppies can start learning to potty on grass by following Mom. They will sniff around, looking for the "right" spot and should be praised gently for success. Before this age, their mother has been cleaning litter messes. She has already taught them to stay clean. Their instinct is to continue being clean.

Owners can introduce a crate containing soft old towels to the nest and play area. The puppies learn to go in and out of the crate, to sleep in it, and to potty away from that area.

Puppies learn quickly during their first 13-16 weeks. They should get lots of individual attention as part of the socialization process.

At four to five weeks, each puppy is taken away from the litter for a few minutes so they can start to learn to be away from mom and littermates. The puppy is returned to the litter before he gets too upset.

Humans can gently start some basic training with the puppies. If the puppies cry or bark wait until the puppy is quiet before responding. These puppies are already learning that barking, whining or crying sends humans away, and quiet brings them closer. Wait until the puppy is sitting before petting or picking him up. They are learning that sitting gets attention and jumping up does not. This is very hard with puppies. Who doesn't want to pick up a puppy that puts his little front paws on your foot or leg for attention?

Ideally the puppies have been back to their veterinarian for a social visit, their first vaccination and worming, and even a second social visit where the staff plays with and handles them so the puppy does not fear its visits to the veterinarian.

Staying with the mother for at least seven weeks is vital for best results in a puppy's life. During that last week, a puppy starts to learn that nipping mom and littermates with those sharp teeth hurts if he uses too much pressure. His littermates walk away, isolating the biting puppy. He learns to soften his bite (called bite inhibition), so the others will continue to play. During that last week, he also learns that mom is not the big softy he thought she was. She can and will growl, snarl, snap, and even bite him if his behavior is too rough or otherwise inappropriate. From this experience with her, he should begin to learn to be appropriate with other adult dogs, although it is likely the puppy will need several experiences with adult dogs to learn not to jump, bite, or chew on them.

At eight weeks, puppies can start going to their new homes although many expert breeders may keep the toy and smaller breed puppies longer, partly because they are just so tiny.

How to Condition a Puppy to Handling

Puppy Training

The ARL – Iowa stresses puppy training classes for the future of the dog and owner.

Statistically, it is very rare for a dog who has participated in a puppy training class to be relinquished by its owner to a shelter.

At 4-5 weeks, puppies should be taken away from the litter for a few minutes of handling each day in preparation for weaning.

Staying with the mother for at least 7 weeks is vital. During that last week, the puppy learns from his mother and littermates that nipping and rowdy behavior is inappropriate.

Seven to Ten Weeks

Now in their new home, puppies are learning quickly and need to meet many people to help them learn to enjoy being around people. Simple, positive training should be started, ideally in a well-run class with a few other puppies of similar age for socialization. When you attend a puppy class you will probably be doing as much listening as training. The instructors will try to answer any questions you or other participants have. Trading successes, tips, and frustrations can be very beneficial for you as well as your puppy.

Basics like Sit and Lie Down can be taught and reinforced very quickly at this age. Puppies are very willing learners and eager to be with their humans. Remember the attention span can be pretty short, so be patient and use frequent short sessions at home.

Overlapping this stage is another stage that runs from about eight weeks through eleven weeks. It is commonly called a fear imprint period. If the puppy reacts to an experience with fear or anxiety, the owner needs to respond and help the puppy become less fearful. For example if a child accidentally steps on a puppy, the puppy might react with fear, even to the point of growling or bolting. If possible (and if the puppy is not seriously hurt) the puppy should be brought back to the child, and using gentle voices, treats and toys, reintroduced to the child in a very positive way. **Anything that happens to the puppy, whether traumatic or positive can have a lasting effect.** Every effort to make life experiences fun is a great investment in the puppy's future.

By ten weeks, puppies are eager to be with their humans and can be taught basic cues such as sit or lie down.

Ten to Sixteen Weeks

From ten to sixteen weeks, puppies are starting to get new teeth. They use their mouths and teeth extensively to explore their environment and to help ease the discomfort of the new teeth erupting. They may try biting you or other pets to try to get their way. This is the age where a new owner becomes grateful for the puppy's eighth week with the mother and littermates. This is when the puppy has learned biting is not acceptable. Lots of structure and gentle but consistent leadership and supervision will get you through this teething stage. Refer to "Nothing In Life Is Free" in Chapter 8. Also continued socialization with other puppies and dogs teaches your puppy what is and is not acceptable.

Troubleshooting

If you are concerned that your puppy's behavior seems excessive or he is growling or biting, you may want to call an experienced trainer or behavior expert for help.

Continued socialization with other puppies and dogs teaches appropriate behavior.

Importance of Training

Dogs that have not had the benefit of training and socialization before adulthood are the ones that often get turned into shelters.

We get calls from owners who are having problems with dogs that have suddenly become territorial, protective, or have started guarding their toys, food bowl, bed, and even their humans from other dogs and people. They are described as not trainable, hyper, vicious, suddenly aggressive, and various other descriptions that usually indicate poor socialization and lack of training. These dogs have stayed in their home because as puppies they were cute and cuddly, but, as adults without guidance, structure and training they appear dangerous to their owners.

Puppies are now starting to be brave about leaving you. If you think your puppy has been successfully trained not to leave your side, this is the age you will find out they are willing to wander off, leaving you for more exciting scents, sights, and sounds. Many puppies become lost at this age (hopefully just temporarily), because they are testing the boundaries. You want to make sure they are safely confined when outside. Never leave a puppy tied up outdoors unsupervised.

There is a time in a puppy's life where they seem to have "puppy license" to get away with some naughty behaviors with other dogs. Many adult dogs, especially males, it seems, will tolerate puppy biting, jumping, climbing, tail pulling, and other obnoxious behaviors that the dog would not allow from another adult dog. Usually, at about five to seven months, this puppy license "expires". The adult dogs start to treat the puppy like a juvenile delinquent and will stop rude puppy behaviors.

When an adult dog stops allowing these behaviors, many owners misinterpret what the adult dog is doing. The adult may look like he is going to hurt the puppy and the puppy often squeals, falls on his back and acts like he is being hurt. As scary as this scenario is, your puppy needs to know the boundaries with adult dogs. This is a lesson he will remember. Scolding or punishing the adult dog that is just doing his job training the puppy is a mistake. It can literally turn your puppy into a bully.

Sixteen Weeks to Eight Months

At some time between sixteen weeks and eight months, most puppies go through a "flight instinct" period, also commonly called a testing period. This is the time a puppy seems to have forgotten housetraining, manners and anything else previously taught. He might bite, run, pretend to be deaf and ignore any efforts to rein him in. *This is an adolescent stage that can break bonds with you if you aren't aware that it is TEMPORARY.*

Your sweet puppy will come back. The stage usually lasts only one or two weeks, even though it seems permanent. Many physical changes occur; your puppy is growing so fast during this time. Remember he is still teething with the big molars coming in. He may be having pain and discomfort. He is still a puppy. He needs structure, love, and training. Don't forget exercise, as his needs for games and stimulation will grow during this time. New toys may be destroyed in minutes so tougher toys should be used. Playtime with other compatible puppies and dogs should be maintained but carefully supervised, using one- or two-minute time outs if he gets too rough.

Overlapping this stage is a second fear stage that often occurs between six months and fourteen months. Sometimes puppies that have never shown fear of strangers, dogs, or places will exhibit fear now. Even with familiar people, the puppy may suddenly be unfriendly, growl, and show fear. Continue classes. Keep training using a gentle voice, treats and toys and be positive, but avoid forcing the issue if the puppy shows fear.

Wait a couple of weeks to introduce him to new people, but continue practicing what he has learned in situations where he is fearful. If you act very "matter of fact" and expect him to be too, it can help get him through this stage. Just don't punish him when he is afraid or be disappointed if he can't perform now as he did before. Reward any effort on his part. Help him be successful, even if you are stepping back in your training to an earlier phase. Praise and reward his efforts during this period.

Adulthood: Twelve Months and Older

A puppy is considered an adult from one year on, even though many dogs don't mentally or emotionally mature until two years of age or even older. Some breeds have individuals that never act "adult," like the Golden Retrievers that are perpetual puppies and are cherished for it.

Unfortunately, once a dog enters a shelter and shows aggressive behaviors he is a concern. How easily this could have been avoided with early training and socialization.

When do you spay or neuter?

Shelters spay or neuter young dogs around 8 weeks of age and always before adoption. Consult your veterinarian on the best time to spay or neuter your pet.

A female will go into "heat" or "estrus" anywhere from 6 months to a year old. If she hasn't been spayed, she can get pregnant during this time. She can even get pregnant at this first heat, so extreme care must be taken. If she is confined outdoors, she must be supervised, as male dogs will be very creative trying to reach her, even climbing fences or digging into kennels.

Male puppies that have not been neutered may start to lift their legs to mark vertical objects, especially if they see other male dogs.

Topics:

Choosing A Puppy

How do you choose a puppy, especially if you are going to purchase one, instead of adopting from a shelter?

- Be sure you are getting a puppy from a reputable source. Check with your veterinarian or ask the breeder who does his veterinary work and talk with him.

- Be sure the puppy has been with the mother and littermates until he is at least eight weeks old.

- Travel to the site where the puppy is living. Be sure to do your research before bringing home any pet.

Purchasing from a breeder

Ethical, responsible breeders will interview you, gathering information that will help you decide if their breed is right for you.

They will insist that if at any time in the life of the dog you get from them, you cannot keep him, you will return him to them, and will have you sign a contract to that effect.

They will either spay or neuter the puppy before you take him home, or insist you sign a contract to have the dog spayed or neutered at a later date. They will provide information on training, house training and other details specifically about that breed.

They will have already screened the parents, grandparents and previous generations for genetic defects that can affect the lifespan and quality of life for your puppy. Every breed has genetic factors that responsible breeders attempt to avoid or selectively breed away from. A good breeder will have raised the puppies in the middle of their own family, exposing the puppies to children, other dogs and pets, and to routine family life.

Choosing a Puppy *Continued*

They will have begun house training.

They will have taken the puppies to a veterinarian for exams, preliminary vaccinations. and worming. They will provide you with that information for your vet.

They will be pleased when you ask questions, and they will have good answers. They will want to see how you and your family respond to their dogs, even the mother and father of the puppies. They will want to see how your children are with the puppies.

Does the breeder insist the puppies stay with the mother and litter through eight weeks? This is so vital to the behavior of the puppies, yet such a common problem with casual or backyard breeders. Keeping puppies with their mother gives her the chance to teach them to "mind their manners". Keeping the litter together through eight weeks lets the puppies learn from each other that it hurts when they bite too hard and nobody will play with them. This is an important social lesson for puppies. When the pups don't learn this lesson before the age of twelve weeks, they can become difficult for families to live with. Teaching it at an older age is much more difficult.

By the same token, a puppy that is an "only child" can have the same behavior issues if care is not taken to be sure he is socialized.

It is our understanding that no ethical or reputable breeder would offer puppies to a broker or middle man to be sold at pet stores or online.

Just the right dog or puppy may be in a shelter waiting for you.

Choosing a Puppy *Continued*

Adopting From a Shelter

When looking for a dog, check your local shelter. Shelter dogs come in all breeds, ages, sizes, colors, characteristics, abilities and temperaments. They come from a variety of sources, pet stores, breeders, newspaper ads, friends and neighbors who have an occasional or accidental litter and need to find homes for puppies.

In 2010, approximately 19 percent of dogs obtained to be family pets were adopted from a shelter. While that is not a bad number, the shelter world wants to see that number increased since there are four- to- six- million dogs and cats that never find homes and are euthanized.

Shelters receive puppy litters of both purebred and mixed breeds. Puppies are often cared for in foster homes until ready for adoption.

Avoid Buying A Puppy Mill Puppy

What is a PUPPY MILL and what can we do about them?

Puppy mills are breeding businesses which mass produce litters of puppies for profit.

The breeding dogs are often housed in cages with wire floors and unsanitary conditions with little to no attention paid to their physical or social well-being.

The mother dogs are bred and re-bred repeatedly until no longer profitable. Puppies are sold directly to pet stores or marketed on-line. Often the puppies have genetic problems due to sloppy breeding and socialization problems due to the lack of early human contact.

Sadly, puppy mills are not illegal. Those that sell wholesale to pet stores are subject to USDA regulations but the system is not sufficient to quickly address suffering. Plus, there is a huge loophole. Puppy mills that sell directly to the public, for example over the internet, are not currently covered by federal and state requirements.

Due to the abuses uncovered in puppy mills, all animal welfare advocates support additional federal and state regulations to ensure adequate veterinary care, food, water, cleaning and housing of breeding animals, and, support active investigation and litigation to shut down those operations that abuse and/or neglect animals.

What YOU can do about puppy mills.

ALWAYS obtain your puppy or dog:

- from an animal rescue and shelter organization (or through in-store pet adoptions offered by a reputable animal shelter).
- from an experienced, reputable breeder that you can visit in person or whose reputation is reliably confirmed.
- through a breed-specific rescue group.
- Do NOT purchase a dog or puppy from an online seller without seeing the kennel conditions and meeting the mother dog.
- If you see evidence of abuse or neglect at a kennel in your area, contact your local shelter or state humane society for advice on how to proceed.

Some happy endings
from the Animal Rescue League of Iowa

Nettie

In 1983 I adopted my first pet from the ARL, a little mixed breed dog named Murphy. Since that time I have adopted other pets, all from the ARL. All of them have their own unique story, but the story of Nettie, my current dog, stands out as a testimonial to the successful work the ARL does with animals in need and the impact of that work on one dog's life.

Nettie, along with many other Golden Retrievers, came to the ARL in 2004 as the result of the closure of a puppy mill. She was two years old and used to breed many litters. She spent her days with little human contact, trying to alleviate boredom by chewing on the chain link fencing she was enclosed in. After arriving at the ARL, the staff worked with her and slowly the dog she was meant to be emerged.

Today, Nettie is a certified therapy dog. The care she was given during her stay with the ARL has not only made a difference in her life, but is now making a difference in the lives of the people she touches. Nettie is truly a success story made possible only by her new beginning at the ARL.

Kathy

Keep in mind that choosing the right puppy is quite different from choosing the right adolescent/adult dog.

Visit a shy puppy away from his littermates, so you can see his personality.

Tip: To avoid making a hasty decision, leave the children at home when you make your first visit to a breeder or shelter. Screen the puppy or dog before the kids meet him.

What Are You Looking For?

When you enter a shelter, you will want to have some idea of what type of dog you are looking for.

If you don't have a basic plan or idea of the type of dog that will work in your home, you could make an impulsive choice you will regret.

Looking at those sad and needy eyes in the kennels can be a challenge. Walking away from them is heart-wrenching. If you do have room for a dog in your home, here are some ideas to help you make a good choice to ensure your pet becomes a permanent part of your family. Keep in mind that choosing the right puppy is quite different from choosing the right adolescent/adult dog.

Genetics

Knowing the genetics of the puppy may be important if you have a specific task in mind for him. However, if he will live his life with you as a pet, going to the park and playing ball or being a couch potato, his parentage may not be an issue.

Sometimes puppies are available for adoption from known parents, or at least, the mother may be known. Litters of puppies can have more than one father, so even in one litter of puppies, there can be a huge variation of the same breed, size, and personality of the puppies.

Another interesting factor is a mixed breed mother, bred with a mixed breed father, can have puppies that do not look anything like either one of them.

While there is something to be said for both nature and nurture on how any particular puppy turns out, nature does rule in some areas. A Border Collie puppy and an English Springer Spaniel puppy will react very differently toward a sheep. The Spaniel may kiss it or try to get it to play with a toy, but the Border Collie will instinctively attempt some form of herding behavior.

What Puppy or Dog Is Right for You?

Consider the following points:

Where do you live? A city apartment? Surburban home? In the country? Your home and lifestyle are important considerations.

What size dog are you comfortable with? What size of dog best fits your home space?

What activity level? Do you have the time to exercise an energetic small dog? An energetic large dog?

Sometimes smaller breeds are more active than larger ones. Retired Greyhounds are among the calmest. Many people think they are high-strung, nervous and need extensive daily exercise, but that is seldom the case. They tend to be calm couch potatoes who enjoy a nap and a walk.

As calm as retired Greyhounds can be, fifteen-pound Terriers can need lots of activity, such as retrieving, playing with other dogs or hunting. If bored and alone, they can become destructive. Shelter staff can help guide you.

Coat care/shedding/professional grooming? Do you have a few minutes several days a week to brush and comb your dog? If not, you should look for a dog with minimal coat care. Larger breeds might be Dalmatians, German Shorthair Pointers and Great Danes. Smaller breeds include smooth-coated Dachshunds, Toy Fox Terriers and Chihuahuas. A quick bath once in a while and a quick comb-through to collect the shedding hair a couple times a week can keep the shedding to a minimal level.

Medium coated dogs like Irish Setters, Border Collies, Labradors and Golden Retrievers need some weekly tending. Poodles, several breeds of Terriers like Airedales and Schnauzers, lap dogs like Shih Tzus, Lhasa Apsos and mixes of all these may need regular professional grooming. The cost and frequency of professional grooming are things to factor into your budget before selecting a breed.

We often get dogs surrendered that are badly matted, have injuries to their skin, infected ears and other problems, all because owners underestimated the costs of grooming.

What about noise? Do you want a dog that is quiet or one that barks?

Male or female? There are lots of opinions, and, like most of the other choices, it comes down to personal preference.

Adopting a wonderful older dog is sometimes the better decision for a family.

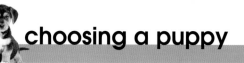
Information About Breeds

Animal Planet, the American Kennel Club, and many other websites can help answer your questions when you are deciding on what breed or breeds might be a match for your situation. It is a fun and good starting point.

Personality

You have made a decision about the type of dog you want and the shelter has a litter of puppies that might fit your criteria. So, out of eight puppies in the litter, how do you decide which one is best for you? Personalities of puppies in the same litter can be dramatically different.

Most shelters do not allow the public in the pens, so look for a puppy trying to make eye contact, being social and working for attention while getting closer to you.

Pick up a puppy, hold him so you can look into his eyes, and evaluate his response.

If some of the puppies are shy when they are in the group, don't automatically rule them out. Visiting with them separately can give them a chance to show their personality without the competition of their littermates. Pups that are demanding or jumping up at you while in the pen can turn out to be quite shy and nervous when meeting with you outside their pen. Puppies need to be brought out of their comfort zone to see how they adjust to new people and environments.

Information About Breeds *Continued*

He might try to lick your face, or he might freeze and seem to go stiff, get frantic and panicky or even urinate out of fear. If he does show fear, does he recover in a few seconds, making up to you, maybe licking, wagging and interacting? If he shows fear and nothing you do seems to help, we recommend meeting another puppy.

If you want a project that needs special care, training and socialization, and may never act like a "normal" dog, the shyest pup may be your dog. If you want a running buddy, ready to rumble or wrestle at the drop of the hat, the boldest pup of the litter might be for you.

In general, for the average family, look for a puppy that is cuddly, outgoing and interested in being near you but not obnoxious. The way a pup interacts helps create the bond that lasts a lifetime.

Evaluating Puppies

Keep in mind the evaluations done with puppies do not guarantee what their personalities will be like when they are grown. No one has been able to devise an evaluation for puppies that consistently predicts their adult personality and talents. Genetics plays a part, as does socialization before and after weaning from the mother and littermates.

Bottom line—choosing a puppy is a bit of a guessing game. If you have firm and definite needs or desires to meet, such as size restrictions, you will want to consider an older dog.

Dog Tales

Susan's family adopted a Border Collie from a Craig's List ad. Susan and her husband had two children and she watched other children in her home after school.

The dog, Dodger, had lived in a home with two graduate students. The students thought they needed to find Dodger a new home because they would be going back to school and wouldn't be home much.

Susan called me concerned that the dog was threatening children.

While the effort to find Dodger a new home sounded good at first, and everyone meant well, when more the of details became known, it was not a good match. The Border Collie had never been alone much, had not been raised around children and had never been crated. Given a Border Collie's energy level, herding instincts and activity needs, and learning that Dodger hadn't been around children, it was clear that this was not a good match.

The students took Dodger back and everyone learned a lesson.

Information About Breeds *Continued*

Adopting an Older Dog

Adopting an older dog has many advantages. You will be able to spend some time with the dog and know for certain how big he is and always will be. You will be able to see if he is friendly, has fears that need to be worked on, needs obedience training or if he will need hours of exercise each day. In general, you will be able to tell WHO HE IS.

Adopting a puppy is fun. The puppy is cute and makes us smile. Adopting the older dog means missing out on that cute "baby" stage. With the older dog, you can make a rational, less emotional decision, but it can be just as much a "love at first sight" experience.

Older dogs are usually at the shelter because a caring owner had no other choice. A shelter dog over age three is likely to be a pretty good dog. If he weren't, he likely would have lost his home long before age three. He was probably a house dog, is housetrained, has been around people and simply needs a home. He likely would be a great addition to a family.

Sometimes these dogs are overlooked because people hesitate to fall in love with a dog they might not have for many years. They miss the opportunity to enjoy these dogs and enrich their own lives.

Jerry came to the ARL to find a new dog after his long-time animal companion died. The dog shown here, Romeo, had been surrendered to the ARL. This photo was taken of them just after they met in an ARL-Hug Room.

In just a few short minutes, Jerry and Romeo formed one of those instant bonds that every dog-lover understands. You can see it in their smiles.

Selecting A Purebred Pooch

Where do you start looking for a purebred puppy or dog? Begin by checking at your local shelter. Nationwide, about thirty percent of dogs and puppies in shelters are purebred dogs. We have had many purebred puppies surrendered. You have the opportunity to adopt a purebred puppy that needs a home just as much as a mixed breed pup.

If the shelter doesn't have the breed you want, check The American Kennel Club website and breeder websites. Refer to page 48 to know what to expect from a reputable breeder. Research the breed rescue websites. The rescue groups often will spell out the reality of living with that breed, even to the extent of trying to talk you out of it. They want people to know the facts before taking one of their dogs home.

After sifting through all the details of a breed and finding a breeder that might have puppies or locating a shelter with a litter you might want to visit, how in the world do you not fall in love with the first puppy you meet?

One main tip—do not take the kids along for the first look. Screen the possible pups before the kids see them. It is wise not to fall for the smallest, cutest, shyest or most outgoing.

For a family with kids, you want a puppy somewhere in the middle. Remember, a shy puppy will be a project, but the outgoing puppy may be more attitude than you are looking for. You want a puppy that comes up to you readily, solicits attention by being near you or licking your hand. You want a puppy that is comfortable when you pick him up, does not scream, urinate or freeze. The puppies that do not fit into this box aren't bad puppies, but it is a matter of finding the right family.

Research the breeds you are interested in to be sure you choose the right dog for you, your family and your lifestyle.

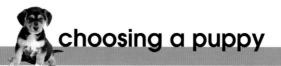

choosing a puppy

Choosing A Breed

From Collies to Corgis and Labradors to Lhasa Apsos, the myriad breeds of dogs tug at your heart.

Are you smitten by the deep pools of their dark eyes, the friendliness of their spirit, or their reputation as steadfast friends? Figuring out where to begin the selection process is a big first step.

Here is a listing of the top 20 most popular purebreds registered to the American Kennel Club for the last few years. It is interesting to see the Labrador has maintained the top spot. Other breeds have been fairly steady, except for Bulldogs and Doberman Pinschers, which have increased dramatically in the last ten years.

BREED	2010	2009	2005	2000
Labrador Retrievers	1	1	1	1
German Shepherds	2	2	4	3
Yorkshire Terriers	3	3	3	7
Beagles	4	5	5	5
Golden Retrievers	5	4	2	2
Bulldogs	6	7	13	21
Boxers	7	6	7	9
Dachshunds	8	8	6	4
Poodles	9	9	8	6
Shih Tzu	10	10	9	10
Rottweilers	11	13	16	11
Miniature Schnauzers	12	11	10	13
Chihuahuas	13	12	11	8
Doberman Pinschers	14	15	21	23
Pomeranians	15	14	14	12
German Shorthaired Pointers	16	16	20	24
Great Danes	17	21	24	28
Siberian Huskies	18	22	25	19
Shetland Sheepdogs	19	18	18	16
Boston Terriers	20	19	17	18

Choosing A Breed *Continued*

There is a mix of large and small breeds, some with short coats, a few with coats that need regular grooming, but only two heavy-coated breeds, the Siberian Husky and the Shetland Sheepdog, appear in the top 20. Also, as urbanized as much of America has become, the number of large breeds is a surprise. You can look up your favorite breeds listed on www.akc.org.

Of course, the mixed breed, or "All American Dog," is really number one, but mixed breeds aren't registered or recognized by a national registration group.

LABRADOR RETRIEVER

GERMAN SHEPHERD

YORKSHIRE TERRIER

MIXED BREED

Choosing A Breed *Continued*

Those Beautiful Breeds

Most dog breeds are listed by the American Kennel Club (AKC) and are divided into groups, which include: Toy breeds, Terriers, Working, Sporting, Non-Sporting, Hounds, and Miscellaneous.

The American Kennel Club is the club most people think of when they want to obtain a "registered" dog. It has a website, www.akc.org, where breeders, local training clubs, and breed rescue groups are listed.

Most pet dogs come from the Sporting Group or the Herding Group. But you probably know dogs that live with family and friends from each group, including Miscellaneous.

According to the AKC, dog breeds are sorted by the kennel clubs according to their work, size, or abilities but then again, sometimes they aren't. For example, in Toy breeds there are several terriers, including Yorkshire Terriers, Silky Terriers and Toy Fox Terriers. These breeds have recent ancestors that were used for hunting and killing vermin. In more recent years, the size has been bred smaller to appeal to the house dog market, yet much of the instinct in these dogs still drives them to hunt and can make them tricky to live with because of their high activity level.

We will talk a bit about dog groups in general. For in-depth information, go to individual breed websites to learn about coat care, general temperament, history of the breed and other common traits.

Approximately thirty percent of dogs and puppies in shelters nationwide are purebred dogs.

Herding Group

A popular group is the Herding Group, which includes Collies, Border Collies, Australian Shepherds, Australian Cattle dogs and many more breeds you will recognize. Many of these breeds are multiple purpose dogs. They are a great choice for dog sports or working dogs, such as search and rescue and service work.

Pros: Herding Group dogs are fun, energetic, eager to learn and good with older children.

Possible Cons: Some in this group have coats that need a lot of coat care. Most need exercise and training to keep them calm and out of trouble in the house.

AUSTRALIAN
SHEPHERD

BORDER COLLIE

COLLIE

WELSH CORGI

OLD ENGLISH
SHEEP DOG

GERMAN SHEPHERD

AUSTRALIAN
CATTLE DOG

BEARDED COLLIE

BRITTANY

COCKER SPANIEL

GOLDEN RETRIEVER

LABRADOR

ENGLISH POINTER

VIZSLA

WEIMARANER

SPRINGER SPANIEL

Choosing A Breed *Continued*

Sporting Group

The majority of pets come from the Sporting Group that includes Labrador Retrievers, Golden Retrievers, Setters, and Spaniels. While hugely diverse in size, body type, and coat type, they were all purposely bred for working with hunters or wildlife guardians.

Today many of these breeds are divided between the "show" bloodlines and the "working" bloodlines. What this means is when you are looking to add a Labrador puppy to your family, you might want to research the parents. Dogs that are bred as "field" labs will have a much higher energy level, endurance level, and need to be exercised and trained more than those dogs that are bred for the show ring. If possible, you will want to meet the parents.

Sporting dogs do well with several hours of training and work each day. A walk around the block is not enough. Putting them into an exercise program makes them more fit and stronger. Training, work, and more training makes them happy, calm, and easier to live with.

By far, the majority of working police, bomb-sniffing, and drug dogs are from field Labrador bloodlines. Also, many service dogs, including leader dogs for the blind, are labs or mixes. These dogs are usually purpose-bred, meaning the parents are bred and kept for breeding more leader dogs.

Dogs trained for the hearing impaired are often shelter dogs, specially selected for traits useful for that work.

The show bloodlines can be tricky, as the show dogs are bred for looks and not necessarily for temperament. Temperament in dogs is definitely affected by genetics. Breeding dogs to get a particular color, tail length, eye shape, or ear set can short-change the dog on personality and temperament. Some are still wonderful, but others can be short-tempered, and unpredictably aggressive. For example, a popular English Springer Spaniel won so many dog shows that he was used as a stud for many puppies. The trouble was, he had an apparently inherited trait that could cause unpredictable aggressive behavior. Some, if not many, of the puppies displayed the trait to the point that "Springer Rage" became a diagnosis for their aggressive behavior.

Pros: Sporting Group dogs are easy to train, bred to work closely with humans, and they listen to instructions. They have lots of natural instincts that are easily modified to working dogs and dog sports stars. They are generally tolerant of children and can be great family pets.

Many of these breeds have "field" types and "conformation" types. Their personalities and exercise needs can be vastly different. You will want to attend classes when these dogs are young. They can be destructive if bored or under exercised.

Possible Cons: Sporting dogs are active, athletic dogs even as puppies and adolescents. They do shed. They may have a genetic drive to hunt. A long quiet walk in a field may be interrupted by chasing squirrels, pointing birds, or running after deer.

Dog Tales

Picking the Right Dog

Teddy was a huge polar bear of a Great Pyrenees dog, with lots of hair and lots of energy. He got along with some dogs, not as well with others, and with the other details like daily brushing, shedding, cost of food, and veterinary care, he was a little hard to find just the right home for. Many Great Pyrenees are calm dogs, never needing much more than a walk around the block, but Teddy loved toys, was much more active than the others we had adopted out, and needed a home that could take on all his needs.

Along came an adopter, a nice lady with a fenced yard and experience with Collies so she knew about shedding hair. Divorced a few years ago, she was ready to bring a new dog into her life. She loved Teddy, played with him, walked him, and spent about half a day deciding to adopt him. She returned him before we closed that same night! Why?

When she got him home, he grew! He seemed much bigger in her home than he had at the shelter. While this may seem ridiculous, it has happened enough times that we actually warn people that the giant breed dogs will seem bigger when they get them home. Teddy came back to us, no harm done, lady embarrassed, but we found him a home with people who had already had several giants, including Saint Bernards and Newfoundlands. They were thrilled because Great Pyrenees tend to be much less "drooly" than the breeds they had before.

BASSET HOUND

BEAGLE

DACHSHUND

WHIPPET

BLOODHOUND

IRISH WOLFHOUND

**RHODESIAN
RIDGEBACK**

SALUKI

Choosing A Breed *Continued*

Hound Group

This group includes a varied mix. Some are the so-called sight hounds, like Greyhounds, Irish Wolfhounds, and Scottish Deerhounds. Others are scent hounds, like Beagles, all the Coonhounds, Bloodhounds, and Basset hounds. This group includes the tallest breed, Irish Wolfhounds, and some small breeds, such as Miniature Dachshunds.

Dachshunds pretty much have their own show, as they come in miniature and standard (bigger) sizes and three coat types: smooth, long-coated and wire-coated.

Some of the rare breeds in this group include Borzoi, Ibizan hounds, and PBGVs (Petit Basset Griffon Vendeen). The PBGV looks a bit like a long-haired Basset hound.

Pros: This group offers variety in size, personality, and coat type, something for everyone. The Scent hounds can be wonderful family pets, tolerant, and loving with children. The Sight hounds are also loving and incredible pets.

Possible Cons: The Scent hounds tend to use their incredible noses constantly, so going for a walk can get frustrating, as they attempt to capture every scent.

The Sight hounds are bred for endurance; that is, to run for a long time. Many have no sense of fences, roads, or other obstacles when they run, so they can be injured or lost easily and should be carefully contained on a leash or in enclosures they are familiar with.

Choosing A Breed *Continued*

Non-Sporting Group

Non-sporting dogs are a mixed group, with the Poodle (miniature) and Bichon Frises included with the Bulldogs and Dalmatians.

Pros: Many of this breed are popular family dogs. With their small to medium size, they are easy to take along on family outings. Because it is such a mixed group, it is hard to discuss this group of dogs in generalities.

Possible Cons: Several are considered "northern" breeds with heavy coats that take a lot of care and brushing. Some have less attentive personalities, like the Chow Chows and Keeshonds. Several are Asian breeds, like the Shiba Inus, Lhasa Apsos, and Shar Peis. Several in this group should be considered carefully before bringing into a family with children.

AMERICAN ESKIMO

BOSTON TERRIER

BULLDOG

SHAR-PEI

CHOW

DALMATIAN

KEESHOND

LHASA APSO

NORWEGIAN ELKHOUND

POODLE

BICHON FRISE

CAVALIER KING CHARLES

CHIHUAHUA

MALTESE

PEKINESE

SHIH TZU

YORKSHIRE TERRIER

TOY FOX

MINIATURE POODLE

PUG

MINIATURE PINSCHER

Choosing A Breed *Continued*

Toy Group

The Toy group is fun, and these dogs are often considered "purse" dogs since they can be carried in a large shoulder bag. Some are furry like Pomeranians, Maltese, and Toy Poodles, and some are smooth coated, like the Toy Fox Terriers and Miniature Pinschers. Some come in several coat types, like Chihuahuas, where you can get a smooth coat or a long-haired type. Many of these breeds need regular professional coat care, so take that into consideration when researching them.

Pros: Toy Group dogs are small in size and generally good with children, if raised around gentle kids. There is lots of variety in coat types and looks, from Toy Poodles to the Toy Fox Terriers. Temperaments and needs of this group vary greatly, and these dogs tend to be personable lap dogs and good travelers.

Possible Cons: The Terriers need training and lots of socialization with children, other pets, and strangers. The Chinese Cresteds and Italian Greyhounds have little to no coat, and can be fragile to handle, even to the point of breaking a leg in every day life, for no particular reason. Several of the breeds have coats that need professional grooming, so budget that factor into owning one of them.

Terrier Group

The Terrier group includes Bull Terriers, Miniature Schnauzers, and Airedales. These breeds are smart, fun, and feisty, but all take some endurance and an owner with some attitude to keep up with and train them. Bred to hunt and kill, they can be too tough to have around young children without one hundred percent supervision.

The Bull Terriers can be intentionally funny, clownish dogs. They have a reputation of being difficult to train, but get them interested and use the right motivation and they can be fun and entertaining. Airedales are giant Terriers and have all the fun-loving personality of the smaller Terriers, but they can look you in the eye. If you like a fun, strong-minded dog in a bigger package, this could be the dog for you.

Miniature Schnauzers have been in the commercial pet market for years. Those that have been bred for temperament instead of the retail market are beautiful, intelligent, personable, and so fun to train. They need regular professional grooming.

Possible Cons: Terriers, more than most dogs, will take on the responsibility of alerting the household to strangers, postal carriers, package delivery people, skateboarders, dogs, squirrels, and bugs. They will take on any reason to bark, unless the owner is on the ball and gives them something else to do.

AIREDALE

AMERICAN PIT BULL TERRIER

BULL TERRIER

CAIRN TERRIER

FOX TERRIER

WEST HIGHLAND TERRIER

SCOTTISH TERRIER

MINIATURE SCHNAUZER

Chapter 4 — choosing a puppy

AKITA

MALAMUTE

BOXER

DOBERMAN

GREAT PYRENEES

SAMOYED

HUSKY

SCHNAUZER

MASTIFF

Choosing A Breed *Continued*

Working Group

Some of the most popular Working Group dogs include Bernese Mountain dogs, Doberman Pinschers, Great Pyrenees, St. Bernards, Newfoundlands, and Great Danes. Others in this group include Anatolian Shepherds, Leonbergers, German Pinschers, and Tibetan Mastiffs. This group is an interesting mix of extra large and large dogs, and most of the "giant" breeds are included here.

Possible Cons: Some of these breeds are intended to work independently of their human caretakers. For example, Kuvasz, Komondor and Great Pyrenees are livestock guarding dogs and some of them live with flocks of sheep to protect them from predators. Some breeds are meant to pull sleds or freight and their urge is to pull away from their caretakers. Several of the breeds are designed specifically for military or police work like Doberman Pinschers and Black Russian Terriers.

Keep in mind that larger dogs often have shorter lifespans. Some of these breeds are known to be vulnerable to genetic problems like cancer and orthopedic issues, such as hip dysplasia. Some of the breeds are rare in the United States, so getting a puppy can be expensive. The rarer breeds have a small gene pool and might be susceptible to inherited problems or temperament problems. When breeders breed for one specific trait, like coat color or size, the temperament of the parents might be less desirable. There is also a lot of shedding in this group.

PUGGLE

'Designer Dogs'

You would think with the amazing variety of size, coat type, temperament and working ability found in the purebred dog world, people would find something that suits them just fine. Lately, however, there has been a "designer" dog fad. Here are some common ones with the purebred parents listed:

Aussie Poo – Australian Shepherd/Poodle
Beagapoo – Beagle/Poodle
Bish-Poo – Bichon Frise/Poodle
Boxerdoodle – Boxer/Poodle
Cairnoodle – Cairn Terrier/Poodle
Cavapoo – Cavalier King Charles Spaniel/Poodle
Chi-Poo – Chihuahua/Poodle
Cockapoo – Cocker Spaniel/Poodle
Doodleman Pinscher – Doberman/Standard Poodle
Doxipoo – Dachshund/Poodle
English Boodle – English Bulldog/Poodle
Eskapoo – American Eskimo Dog/Poodle
Goldendoodle – Golden Retriever/Poodle
Jackapoo – Jack Russell Terrier/Poodle
Labradoodle – Labrador Retriever/Poodle
Lhasapoo – Lhasa Apso/Poodle
Malti-Poo – Maltese/Poodle
Papoo – Papillion/Poodle
Pekepoo – Pekingese/Poodle
Poochin – Japanese Chin/Poodle
Poochon – Poodle/Bichon Frise
Pugapoo – Pug/Poodle
Saint Berdoodle – Saint Bernard/Poodle
Schnoodle – Schnauzer/Poodle
Scoodle - Scottish Terrier/Poodle
Sheepdoodle – Old English Sheepdog/Standard Poodle
Shi-Poo – Shih-Tzu/Poodle
Weimardoodle – Weimaraner/Poodle
Westiepoo – West Highland White Terrier/Poodle
Whoodle – Soft Coated Wheaton Terrier/Poodle

'Designer Dogs' *Continued*

Yorkipoo – Yorkie/Poodle

Beagle Hound – Basset Hound/Beagle

Bichon-A-Ranian – Bichon Frise/Pomeranian

Boglen Terrier – Beagle/Boston Terrier

Beaglier – Beagle/Cavalier King Charles Spaniel

Brat – Boston Terrier/Rat Terrier

Cavachon – Cavalier King Charles
Spaniel/Bichon Frise

Chiweenie – Chihuahua/Dachshund

Chug – Chihuahua/Pug

Cockalier – Cocker Spaniel/
Cavalier King Charles Spaniel

Cocabichon – Cocker Spaniel/Bichon Frise

Goldador – Golden Retriever/Labrador Retriever

Jack Chi – Jack Russell Terrier/Chihuahua

Jackabee – Jack Russell Terrier/Beagle

Mai-Shi – Maltese/Shih-Tzu

Malti-Pom — Maltese/Pomeranian

Morkie (Malkie) – Maltese/Yorkshire Terrier

Pomchi – Pomeranian/Chihuahua

Peek-A-Pom – Pekingese/Pomeranian

Puggle – Pug/Beagle

Shorkie – Yorkie, Yorkshire Terrier/Shi-Tzu

Silkchon – Bishon Frise/Silky Terrier

Yorkie Apso – Yorkshire Terrier/Lhasa Apso

Yorktese – Yorkshire Terrier/Maltese

Zuchon – Shih-Tzu/Bichon Frise

Most, if not all, of these designer dogs have landed in our shelter with Puggles, a mix of Pugs and Beagles, the most commonly surrendered. If you are looking for a mixed breed designer dog, check a shelter.

Butters   Labradoodle

Scrabble   Goldendoodle

Iowa's "Puppy Mill" law, requires commercial breeders, dealers and public auctions for dogs and cats to obtain a State permit, makes each facility subject to inspection by the State Department of Agriculture and sets minimum standards of care for animal shelters, boarding kennels, commercial breeders, commercial kennels, dealers, pet shops, pounds, public auctions, and research facilities. Minimum standards are defined as "[a]dequate feed, adequate water, housing facilities, sanitary control, or grooming practices, if such lack causes adverse health or suffering" and veterinary care".

Some happy endings
from the Animal Rescue League of Iowa

Oksana

Shortly after passage of "Puppy Mill" legislation, a commercial breeder relinquished 300 dogs to the ARL.

Oksana, a very pregnant Corgi was one of the 300 "breeder" dogs. Karen and the ARL watched over Oksana through delivery. Then, through the ARL's foster-home program, Karen brought Oksana and her puppies home to care for them prior to adoption.

She had seven puppies and Karen considered adopting one. But, Karen fell in love with and adopted Oksana.

Oksana did not like to be touched. She didn't know human contact. She would leave her bed only to eat and be taken outside to potty. She had the habit of walking in small circles—perhaps that was all the space she knew. Her entire life had been spent confined to a 3-foot by 3-foot kennel.

Karen says, "I've had Oksana for about 1-1/2 years. After about 4 months, she started to allow some petting. Now, she is 3/4 normal." Karen continues to work with her. And, as you can see, Oksana may still be a little shy, but she is very happy in her loving home.

Mia

Mia, a mixed breed about 5-1/2 years old, was brought into the ARL by a farmer who said,"She was dumped in my yard."

Mia was full of ticks, 10 in just one ear, and VERY pregnant. She appeared to have lived in the country because she got very nervous with all the "city noises."

Karen and the ARL watched over Mia at the shelter until she had her 8 healthy puppies. Karen then took a healthy Mia and the little family home with her until they were ready to find their new forever homes.

Topics:

Supplies You'll Need

So you have picked out your new family member and are ready to start incorporating him into your household.

Here are some ideas to help make this transition as smooth as possible. We recommend you have some supplies on hand before you bring the dog into your home:

A food bowl and heavy ceramic water bowl

The food bowl won't be on the floor all the time (unless your pet is crated or confined while you are gone). You want a sturdy, non-metallic bowl that doesn't tip easily. A heavy water bowl makes it less likely your dog will put his feet in it or carry it around.

Food

Basic nutritional needs are met with any dog food labeled complete. It is important to remember the first three ingredients listed on the bag make up the majority of the food. The ARL will let you know what food your dog has been eating while there. If your dog has been doing well on this food, you may want to continue it. If you choose to change your dog's food, do your research because the varieties of dog food are endless. Check with your veterinarian if you have questions.

Have the recommended supplies on hand before bringing your dog home.

A collar, leash, microchip and tag

When the Animal Rescue League sends a pet home, he leaves with a collar, leash, microchip and tag with the ARL's ID number and phone number. You may want to purchase a harness for walking your dog. For more control, we recommend the Gentle Leader™ halter.

Crates

Be sure you select the right size crate. There are two main types of crates used for housetraining and confinement, metal-barred folding crates or plastic crates with windows and metal doors. The plastic crates are often used for airline shipping of dogs.

There are also steel crates law enforcement officers and hunters use. Fabric varieties can be used for dogs that are used to being crated and, therefore, won't try to chew or dig their way out. Fabric ones are easily damaged from the inside, so they are never a good choice for a young puppy or a dog that isn't used to it and may be anxious to get out. Refer to Crate Training in Chapter 8 to get your puppy settled, happy and comfortable in a crate.

Bed

A rug or mat is a fine first bed for your puppy. In the ARL kennel area, we offer the Kuranda™ beds for dogs. Some take to the beds just fine, but some ignore them and sleep on the heated tile floor. They are easy to clean, fairly indestructible and useful for our purposes. In a home, you could add padding to make them more comfortable or attractive to your dog. Your local pet store carries a variety of beds to choose from.

Metal folding crate

Plastic crate with windows and metal door

Adding padding to a Kuranda™ bed makes it even more comfortable.

Supervise your dog when he is playing with soft or stuffed toys he can tear.

Choose rawhide made from American hides to avoid toxins and problem chemicals.

Pull toys teach the puppy to chase and catch a toy—and not the child.

Supplies You'll Need *Continued*

Toys

There are many toys available that are safe and useful for keeping pets busy. Kong™ toys come in many sizes, shapes and types. The original Kong™ was shaped like a beehive and made of tough rubber with some give and bounce to it. They are available in several colors, including black ones that are extra tough, and some that show up on X-rays if ingested.

Some will dispense treats or kibble if tipped, so the dog learns to tip it to get the food out. They are a safe way to entertain a puppy and feeding the dog his meals in a Kong™ is a great idea.

Kongs™ are not indestructible, so the first few times you offer them to the dog, supervise to see if he can chew it up. The black color is less likely to be chewed up, so if you bring home a breed with a history of being a strong chewer, like a Pit Bull, Boxer or German Shepherd, choose a black Kong™.

Many people use rawhide for their dogs. Choose rawhide that is labeled made in America or made from American hides. Some rawhide from other sources is processed with toxic or problematic chemicals and can be dangerous to your dog. I like "pressed rawhides," which is a processing technique that seems to be long-lasting and a way to keep the rawhides safer for the dogs. Rawhides should always be supervised toys. Never allow your dog to have them while you are gone.

Supplies You'll Need *Continued*

Toys that are actually puzzles are also available for dogs. These have treats hidden behind small doors on a panel. The key is to find something your dog enjoys and can also engage his mind.

Put out a few toys at a time and rotate them. Keep a few in a drawer and switch them every other day to keep them new for your dog.

Paula Says

I don't recommend tennis balls for puppies, except for supervised play. Many puppies will start to peel the fuzzy outside covering off, and it doesn't digest well.

Kong™ toys are tough and a safe way to entertain dogs who like to chew. Some dispense treats.

Pet Microchip

Every animal adopted from ARL-Iowa has been implanted with a computer microchip placed under the skin between his shoulder blades.

It is a permanent form of identification and every humane society, veterinary clinic and animal control office has a scanner or reader that will show the number on the chip.

One call to an 800 number with that code should get a lost pet back to his owner quickly.

Some breeders offer microchips, too, but be sure to get the details to transfer your puppy's new owner information into the database.

Supplies You'll Need *Continued*

First Aid Kit

Do you know what to do if your pet is choking or if he ate something that might be poisonous?

Check with your local American Red Cross to find out if they offer pet first aid classes. Fill your pet first aid kit with the supplies below and keep it in a handy spot along with these important phone numbers.

- The toll-free number for the Animal Poison Control Center: 888-426-4435.

- Your veterinarian's number and a number for a local emergency or after-hours clinic.

- A copy of your pet's most recent medical records.

- Several rolls of gauze, adhesive tape for bandages, nonstick bandages, towels, or strips of clean cloth.

- A bottle of milk of magnesia and hydrogen peroxide. <u>Do not use these products unless directed by a veterinarian.</u> Using the wrong product could cause more harm than good.

- A digital pet thermometer. These can only be used rectally, but are invaluable if your pet is experiencing heat- or cold-related issues.

- An eye dropper or syringe without the needle for administering medications or fluids, as directed by your veterinarian.

- A muzzle that fits your dog or an old necktie, soft strips of cloth, or a nylon stocking for making a muzzle. If your dog is injured or in pain, he may bite out of fear or pain. The muzzle will keep you safe. I recommend using treats and conditioning to get your dog used to the feel of a muzzle. Then, in an emergency, he is less likely to be even more stressed by the muzzle.

- An extra leash, or several, if you have more than one dog.

If you need to use first aid on your pet, always follow up by contacting your veterinarian for more information or an examination. First aid is not meant to replace veterinary care, but it can save your pet's life, until you can get help from a veterinarian.

Keep the Animal Poison Control Center's and your veternarian's phone number, and, first aid pet supplies handy in case of emergency.

Traveling Home

Keep in mind that the moment you put your new dog in the car to go home, he is learning.

We recommend he be confined in the car from the beginning. It is dangerous for dogs to get on your lap, under your feet, or hang out the window while you are driving. Dogs roaming freely in the car are vulnerable in an emergency. If you hit the brakes or get in a crash, they become flying objects and can be killed going through the windshield or can injure you or your passengers. Dogs can be injured or killed on the roadway if they get out of the vehicle.

People driving and allowing their dogs to hang their heads out the window are putting their pets at risk. Bugs can get in his face, eyes, or ears or if he is leaning far enough out the window, he could be injured by other vehicles or roadside signs.

For safety, be sure your dog is confined in the car when traveling. We recommend a crate.

Moving to a New Home

Pets that are changing locations can experience stress related to moving. Follow the tips below to make the move easier on everyone.

- Keep your dog on his regular schedule before the move. Return to it as soon as possible after moving. The familiarity will reduce his stress level.

- On the day of the move, confine your dog to a familiar room where he feels safe. This will keep him out from underfoot, as well as help him remain calm.

- If at all possible, your dog should be in a crate during the move. Put some of his favorite toys, blankets and something that smells familiar in the crate.

- Make sure any hotels you are planning to stay in will accept pets. Do not leave your dog in the car overnight for any reason.

- When you arrive at your new home, place your dog's food bowl, bed and other items in the same location as his previous home.

- Walk your dog around the house, yard and neighborhood to orient him to his new home.

- Keep an eye on him. Be prepared to deal with any potty accidents without scolding. If you kept your dog on his schedule, accidents should be minimal.

For control, leash your dog before letting him out of the car.

Dog Tales

Microchip Miracle

In the summer of 2005, a man found a tiny Pekingese huddled in the middle of a residential street in Iowa. He brought her to our staff, sure there was an owner looking for her. Little did he know she had been lost from her home in Las Vegas, Nevada, for more than a year.

Her name was Toy, and she was about fourteen-years-old. The microchip that stored her owner information gave us the opportunity to call him. He dropped everything to fly to Des Moines, Iowa, to get her. It was a miracle for Toy and her family, but certainly a mystery that will never be solved. Just how did Toy leave her Las Vegas home and end up in Des Moines? Without a microchip, there would have been no hope of getting her back to the people who loved her.

Traveling Home Continued

First Time Home

When you first arrive home with your new pet, be sure he is on a leash before you open the car door. Many newly-adopted dogs have escaped when owners open the door without realizing the dog may bolt. If the dog is confined in a crate or is on a leash, he can be released from the car with guidance and he will start to learn this is the procedure. Exiting a car should be controlled and carefully supervised. If a puppy, carry him to a potty spot.

- **Select Potty Spot** - Before entering the house, take the dog directly to the potty spot in the yard you want him to use. After an exciting car ride, chances are your dog will need to urinate, and this is the perfect opportunity to set that pattern for him. Take a tour of the house with the dog on a leash. Let him sniff the boundaries and furniture. If he is a male dog he might lift his leg to mark a vertical surface. Clap your hands or make a big "UH! UH!" noise, which will startle him a bit, and you can quickly walk him back to the potty spot outside. Plan on a few trips this way the first hour or so, and it will help him understand the rules. For a puppy, see Chapter 7.

- **Use a Leash** - Even a housetrained adult dog will need supervision and reminders in a new location. Take treats with you when you take the dog out. I recommend taking the dog out on a leash at first, even if you have a fenced yard. Guide the dog to the place you want him to go, and give him a treat or a few minutes of play as a reward for doing his job. If he wants to go back inside, use that as a reward for doing his jobs quickly out-doors. If he wants to do more sniffing and play outdoors, use that as a reward for a quick potty job. You will quickly learn what will be rewarding to your dog, and you can use that to help train other behaviors.

Some dogs that have been allowed to run to the neighbor's yard or away from the house to potty may be reluctant to potty on a short leash with you standing next to him. You might have to try a long ten to fifteen foot line. Ignore the dog, but watch out of the corner of your eye as he wanders around to find the right spot. A quiet bit of praise when he does go will help him learn you want him to go closer to a human than he was used to doing. This can be difficult for some dogs to work through. It is certainly stressful for new owners to try to remedy when the dog won't potty outdoors for them.

- **Supervise** - The first few days in a new home are stressful for any dog or puppy, as well as the owners. In addition to the housetraining protocol, watch to be sure your new pet is chewing on his own stuff and not on your shoes, telephone, remote control, couch, or anything else. Even if he picks up an old shoe you don't care about, trade him for one of his own toys or a treat. Shoes are shoes, and old is the same as new to your dog. Old socks and slippers fall into the same category. Put away items he might be interested in. Keep two or three toys close by so you can help him learn what is okay to play with. Try not to bring a new dog home one day and be gone for eight or nine hours the next. From the dog's point of view, he has been abandoned and some dogs will panic.

If possible take a few days off work, set up a schedule for the dog for housetraining, but also for leaving him alone for short bits of time. Put the dog where he is going to be when you are gone. Pick up your purse or other items you take with you when you leave the house. Count to 50 and come back into the house. Speak quietly and calmly to the dog, no matter what he is doing. Clip a leash to him and take him out to the potty spot. Every time you return, part of the routine should be to take him to that spot. He will start to learn that when you are gone longer and longer, you will still get him outdoors right away, and hopefully he can wait until you get home to go.

Puppy Proof Your Home

Make sure your home is safe for your puppy. Check the location of electrical cords he could chew. A good rule of thumb for housetraining and socializing your new puppy is: crate train him, keep him with you inside and keep him with you outside.

Puppies can't tell the difference between an old shoe and a new one. Trade for a toy!

Keep plenty of toys available and rotate them to keep your dog interested.

Have both dogs on a leash at a safe distance apart when introducing them. Wait for the dogs to establish eye contact before allowing them to come together to meet.

Introducing Your New Dog to Resident Pets

A big consideration before adopting a new dog or puppy is how current pets will receive the new addition to the family?

We can really make a difference in how this transition goes with some tips.

- **Scene one:** Family adopts a second dog and the resident pet has been the only dog for several years.

- **Scene two:** Family adopts a puppy. Resident cat or cats have never met a dog.

- **Scene three:** Resident pets include a cat and an older dog that have gotten along fine for several years. Family has adopted a puppy.

- **Scene four:** Family adopts a kitten. Resident dog or dogs have never been around cats.

While there are many scenes with variations of the above, these are the common ones. Our first priority is safety for all the pets and certainly for the families involved. Our second priority is to keep the stress levels down for everyone. Here are some tips to help get this process started:

1. All dogs are on a leash, whether they are the newly adopted or resident dogs. Ideally, you should have one handler for each dog before the new dog enters the home.

2. All dogs should have met before the adoption was completed, on neutral territory or at the shelter, so compatibility can be determined. Compatibility can change, depending on location, toys, food and the people present. Dogs want to keep their own "stuff" and not let a newcomer have it. That is pretty normal. What we want to determine is will either dog start a fight about the food, toys and other resources? Some growling and posturing is to be expected. Keeping both dogs on leash can help get them out of a tense situation without risking someone putting their hands in the mix.

Dogs meeting naturally without leashes.

3. All humans should do their best to remain calm, keep voices low and keep any excitement out of the situation.

4. Feed the dogs in separate bowls in separate parts of the room or the house. Even dogs that don't guard their food won't like another dog coming around to steal their portion. It is one of the easiest things you can do to prevent friction between dogs.

5. Prepare a safe place for the resident cats so they can escape or get away from the new puppy or dog. It is also a good idea to have the dog on a leash in case you need to prevent him from chasing the cat. This is for the safety of the cat, but it also gives you a chance to help the dog learn to leave the cats alone. Reward and reinforce that behavior.

6. Bringing a new kitten into the home with dogs that are not already "cat savvy" is a big safety concern for the kitten. We recommend keeping the kitten in a large crate in the living area of the house, with space for a bed, litter box, and food and water dishes. Dogs should be outside when the kitten comes home, and until you can get her safely and comfortably settled in the crate. Bring the dogs in, reward them for sniffing, gentle behavior, and ignoring the kitten. **If the dogs become intense, as in stalking or hunting the kitten, you will need a professional to help with this transition.**

We recommend keeping the kitten's living space in the crate until she is old enough and big enough to be able to escape from the dogs, if necessary. This can take a few months.

7. Do <u>NOT</u> scold or punish any of the pets for their behavior. Control, modify, and desensitize them to help them learn to live comfortably with each other. If you have concerns, contact a behavior professional.

If you are bringing hamsters, gerbils, or other small pets home, don't ever leave them alone with your dogs or cats. By nature, dogs and cats are predators, and it will be normal for them to be aroused by the movements, smells and sounds of these tiny animals. Even the most gentle dog or laid-back cat can get into a hunting mode if the opportunity is in front of them.

Have a safe place for your cat to rest while getting acquainted with a new pet.

Sleeping Arrangements

Where will your new pet sleep?

Many pet owners choose to have their dog sleep in a crate, and often that is a good choice, especially since you aren't sure about the dog's potty habits. Confinement is key in helping the dog learn to wait until morning, and sleep through the night. Placement of the crate can make a huge difference for the puppy or dog.

If you are bringing home a puppy that has just been taken from his mother and littermates, isolating him in a crate and putting the crate in a distant spot from your bedroom will make him miserable. Spend some time introducing your puppy to a crate. Use treats and praise (see Crate Training in Chapter 8). Probably feeling abandoned and lonely, he may bark, howl, whine, whimper and generally make noise all night. Just when he settles down, he will hear a noise, and it will start all over again.

If the crate is far enough away from your bedroom, you may not hear the commotion and will be able to sleep, but your pet is miserable. A better option would be to set the crate (or maybe a second crate) in the bedroom of an adult family member. Having a person present doesn't automatically make it okay for the puppy, but a few comforting words can really help. Resist the temptation to take a whimpering, whining puppy out of the crate and into bed with you. Retraining a dog to sleep in a crate after a night or two in a big, cushy bed can be problematic. Puppies will strongly resist being isolated back in the crate, even if you are right beside him in the bed.

Plan on a few nights of interrupted sleep until the puppy understands the routine. Most puppies can sleep through the night at approximately three months of age.

Before that, if he gets restless, sniffs and makes a commotion, it might mean he needs to potty. Carry the puppy to the potty spot, set him down and wait quietly until he goes. Carry him back and put him into the crate. This is not a time for treats or play. Remember you are setting a pattern for the way you want to live with your dog. It is best to keep him in his crate during the night.

A similar set-up can work for older puppies or adult dogs new to your home. If they are isolated far from the sleeping areas, many will bark or howl for hours, looking for company. If they are sleeping in the same room, they will usually be calmer and quiet down more quickly. The other benefit to older puppies and adult dogs is they usually don't have to go outdoors at night.

Set up your new dog's sleeping area near you for comfort, company and quiet.

Suggested Daily Schedule

Early morning—Pick up puppy from crate and head outdoors with a leash and a treat. Put puppy in spot to potty. Success. Give treat and/or play with puppy outside for a couple of minutes. Feed him breakfast in his crate or hand-feed the first ten pieces. Feed the rest in the bowl or scattered on the floor. If the puppy can be outdoors safely for a few minutes, scatter the food in the grass, so the puppy can start using his nose to find it.

After breakfast, put the puppy back in the crate or supervise him for a few minutes until you take him back outdoors for second potty stop. Many puppies need a third trip in the morning to be sure they have done all their jobs, especially if you are leaving for awhile. If you aren't using a crate to confine the pup, keep him on a leash or use an exercise pen set up with toys and a bed. Supervision and confinement will make housetraining much quicker and less stressful for you.

Morning through afternoon—Out to potty every hour or so the first couple weeks. After this, you can start to lengthen the time between trips. Many new pet owners set a timer for an hour to help remember to take the puppy out. Watch for signals from the puppy when he is moving around. If you suspect the puppy will need to go out, don't wait to see, just trust your instinct, and pick him up and go. Always grab a treat and the leash on the way out. If the puppy doesn't do his job, don't give the treat or play with him. Bring him back in, wait a few minutes, and try again. Play time and rewards only come after jobs are done.

Daytime Schedule

7:00 a.m.
- Pick up puppy to potty outside.
- Feed and play.
- Potty.
- Put puppy back in crate.

8-8:30 a.m.
- Take puppy outside to potty.
- More playtime with toys, inside crate or supervised outside crate.
- Take puppy to potty every hour (depending on age).
- Let puppy drink often and watch for sniffing.
- Avoid accidents.

12:00 p.m.
- Feed small lunch.
- Repeat puppy potty routine.

5:00 p.m.
- Feed early supper. Take out.
- Treat and praise when successful.
- Keep puppy awake until bedtime (if possible).
- Take puppy out to potty.

9:00 p.m.
- Crate with comfy toy.
- Listen for restlessness and take out at night if needed.
- Follow the "crate, potty, play, feed, play-crate-potty" routine carefully and your puppy will be trained.

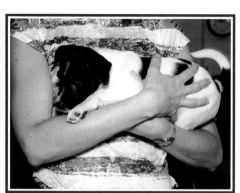

Carry your puppy outside and place him near his 'pee spot'.

When your puppy is successful outside, praise and treat him.

Puppies are clean. They don't want to soil their sleeping/food/play area.

Suggested Daily Schedule *Continued*

For puppies under twelve to sixteen weeks, a lunch meal can be fed, using the same format as breakfast, with two or three trips outdoors before lunch and after lunch.

Late afternoon through bedtime—The evening meal should be fed early enough that the puppy will go outdoors to potty multiple times before crating for bedtime. If the puppy plays hard and drinks a lot of water, take him out more often for an hour or so. Puppies love water and will have to urinate often, with less control. If your puppy is really thirsty, give him some crushed ice. Many dogs love ice, even for treats. Try to keep the puppy awake in the evening. When it is bedtime, put him into the crate with a stuffed toy or something comfy. Listen for restlessness or whining during the night for a quick trip out to potty. Then it is back to his crate and hopefully a quiet night.

You can gradually decrease the number of trips outdoors as your puppy ages and has more control.

Defining Schedules

Adult dog schedules will be a bit different, but the goals are the same.

- It is very individual with each dog, due to his age and history. The biggest difference is adult dogs can hold their urine longer.

- Offer to take your new dog out regularly, and be sure to keep him supervised at all times for a few days.

- When you have to leave him, practice leaving and coming back within a few minutes. We want this dog to know you leave and come back randomly, but you always come back in time.

Sign up for puppy kindergarten with a reward-based trainer.

Outdoor Shelters

If it is necessary to kennel your dogs outdoors, keep these points in mind:

Placement

Place the kennel in close proximity to the house where the dogs will be able to see and hear the family. The owner will also be able to hear if there are any problems with other animals.

Shelter

Dog houses with straw bedding will help keep your pets warm and dry.

Elements

During hot days make sure your dogs have shade, either from a tree or a commercial sun shade. Fans will help to keep the air circulating and a kiddie pool filled with water will provide heat relief as well as entertainment. Always check to see that your dogs have plenty of drinking water.

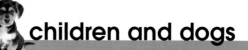
Topics:

Prepping Puppy Before Baby Comes Home

Blending Dogs and Children in the Home

Prepping Puppy Before Baby Comes Home

A Successful Case History

Mike and Mary are newlyweds. Mary has always wanted a dog, so she and Mike start checking ads for puppies. Mary grew up with Rat Terriers and loved their energy and spunk, so she wanted another one in her life.

They found a breeder nearby and went to visit a litter of seven-week-old puppies. The puppies were fat and friendly, and the mother dog was friendly and ready for her pups to start their own life.

The breeder was a farmer who bred his female dog with a neighbor's dog once in awhile. The puppies had been around the grandchildren, were raised in a warm, clean barn, and had been vaccinated by a veterinarian.

Mike and Mary picked out a female and took her home. They named her Molly and took her everywhere. She visited neighbors, friends, and relatives. Mary even took her to work, where she taught kindergarten, so she could meet all the children.

Mike and Mary decided to take Molly to a local training class to learn basic good manners and to be social with other people and puppies. By the time Molly was six months old, she had been around hundreds of people and children, been to classes, loved to play with other dogs and puppies, was almost completely housetrained and was having a wonderful life.

Training classes teach puppies basic good manners and how to be social with other people and puppies.

Little did Molly know her life was about to change. Mary was pregnant and expecting a baby in a few months. Mike and Mary were busy preparing for a new baby, but they wanted to be sure Molly was also prepared for a baby to enter the family. They worried she would feel left out, alone, abandoned, or afraid. They wanted to be sure Molly understood a new baby would be a good thing for her, so they started to prepare Molly for the big event and the huge changes that were about to occur.

First, they had to decide if Molly was allowed in the baby's room. If she was going to be allowed in the baby's room, they did not want her on the furniture, in the crib, or on the changing table. They started to teach Molly to go to her bed on cue. Not only did they work on this trick in the nursery, but everywhere else in the house. They stationed several comfy dog beds around the areas where they would be spending most of their time. Using treats and praise, they taught Molly to go to the nearest bed with a cue word of "go to bed" and Molly learned to settle there until Mike or Mary gave her something else to do. Lots of times she was given a stuffed Kong™ or chew bone while on the bed.

If Mike and Mary had decided Molly wasn't allowed in the nursery, they might have taught her to go to her bed just outside the door, or even exchanged the regular room door for a screen door. That way, Molly could still see and hear them in the baby's room and wouldn't feel as excluded as she would if the solid door had been closed.

Exchanging the regular door on the baby's room for a screen door will keep the puppy from feeling excluded when you are tending to the baby.

The couple kept up Molly's other training, like Lie Down and Stay. They taught Molly to stay at the bottom of the stairs until they called her to come up, so she wouldn't be racing or tripping someone carrying the baby.

They borrowed a doll that made baby noises, bought some powder and lotions they planned to use with the baby, and practiced with the doll so Molly could see the process, sniff the smells and get used to the change in body posture Mike and Mary had when they carried the doll.

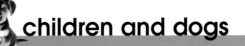

Encourage your dog to retrieve toys so someone can play with her, even if the baby is nearby.

A doll scented with the powders and lotions you plan to use on the new baby will help your dog get used to "baby" smells.

Prepping Puppy Before Baby Comes Home *Continued*

Mike and Mary made sure Molly got some exercise each day, but encouraged her to retrieve toys so someone could play with her, even if the baby was nearby. They practiced her tricks every day, but they also spent some time away from Molly, so she could start to understand they were not as available to her as they had been. It wasn't that Molly wouldn't get attention, play, love, and cuddle time, but it would be on a different schedule, and they wanted to get her used to the changes.

- They practiced praising Molly when she was gentle and calm around the doll.

- They taught her to sniff the doll and then go to her bed.

- They praised and rewarded her for not jumping on them or any visitors.

- They played a CD with crying baby sounds on it, gradually increasing the volume so Molly became used to it and was rewarded for her calm behavior.

- If she showed any concerns, they acted matter of fact about it and played with Molly to help her understand there was nothing to worry about.

- They changed her feeding schedule from having food available at all times to feeding her two meals a day.

- However, they varied the schedule randomly so Molly wouldn't get concerned if the meal was early or late.

- They agreed they would never scold Molly in the presence of the baby. Everything about the baby would be fun, calm and positive for Molly.

Friends and family were surprised that they were keeping Molly after the baby came. Mike and Mary wanted to be able to show how appropriate and trained Molly was.

Prepping Puppy Before Baby Comes Home *Continued*

The next thing Molly knows, Mary is gone for a few days, and comes home with the new baby. Molly takes it all as a usual day, even though there is lots of company and excitement in the house. She has seen it all, smelled it all, experienced it all before, so no big surprises for her.

One year later, Molly is two years old and the baby, Anna, is a year old. Molly's life is very different. Anna is walking, talking, and could be a scary factor in Molly's life. Fortunately, Mike and Mary continued to train and socialize Molly to help her understand toddlers. Toddlers appear very different to dogs as soon as they start to crawl, then walk. They are about eye level with the dog and stumble, cry and speak some strange language. They like to grip puppy tails, ears, paws and noses.

Mike and Mary do a great job supervising Molly and Anna, even putting Molly in another room or outdoors, if they can't supervise them. They also have taught Molly the occasional ear tug or tail grasp is to be tolerated, and have performed these behaviors themselves, pairing the discomfort with treats to help Molly cope.

Always supervise your child and dog.

What they did right

- Decided they wanted a Rat Terrier puppy and looked for one from a breeder. They also could have visited their local shelter to see if any were available for adoption.

- While looking for their puppy, they chose one that was raised with children and was very friendly with them. They made sure the puppies in the litter were at least seven weeks old before separating them from their mother.

- The puppy had been started on vaccinations and worming, so she was less susceptible to viruses that can cause diseases.

- They socialized and trained her starting when she was very young.

- They taught her to stay out of the way, some basic house manners like Stay, or wait at the bottom of the stairs, at the door, and before getting out of the car.

- They prepared the nursery and then started training Molly for her role in the baby's life.

- They prepared her for the baby by showing her a toy "baby" with all the smells and noises that come with a baby. They taught her to be gentle and calm around the doll.

- They prepared her to expect changes in her daily schedule of meals, exercise, and playtime.

- They planned and practiced being positive when the baby was in the room with Molly.

Blending Dogs and Children in the Home

Children and dogs can be amazing.

There is no question they can be good for each other, but there are some key points to consider before bringing a dog into the family home.

- Children do not understand dog language and dogs do not understand a child's language. Adults should supervise their interactions.

- Small children do not understand dog language, even the most obvious things like growling or snapping. You need to teach your child that when a dog is growling or showing his teeth, it may be a sign that he is ready to bite. The child should stop whatever he is doing and freeze. Count to five and slowly, calmly back away from the dog. Do not stare. Do not turn your back to the dog.

Pets and children are a great combination, but keep in mind children do not understand dog language and dogs do not understand a child's language. Supervise your young children and pets at all times.

- Children under the age of seven should be supervised at all times with any dog, even the family dog.

- Dogs do know children run and are fun to chase. Children scream or squeal. They sometimes hit, pinch, or hold on to the body parts of the dog, even if he struggles. Children like to hug dogs, kiss them on the nose, and even blow in their faces.

- Children and dogs both love the game tug-of-war, but it can escalate into a dangerous biting scene, even if done in play, because the dog will regrip his end of the tug. The dog can accidentally move his teeth to a place where fingers are holding on, and grip that spot.

- Teach children never to wrestle with the dog or try to get a toy away from him. Teach them to stay out of the dog's bed and crate, away from the food bowls, unless supervised, and especially to leave the dog alone if he has a bone or toy he is chewing on. A dog will protect the things that are important to him, even to the point of biting. It is helpful to teach your dog to "trade" (see Chapter 8). With "trade" he learns to give up one thing to receive another. This is positive behavior to teach both dog and child.

- Be careful not to do anything to your dog you don't want your children to copy. If your dog isn't great about having his toenails trimmed, wait to trim them when the kids aren't around. We don't want the dog to associate the presence of the children with this task, and you don't want the children to try to trim nails when you aren't watching. Some things your dog will tolerate from an adult won't go as well when children try.

Blending Dogs and Children *Continued*

Sending the kids and dog outdoors to play in the yard happens in families everywhere every day. But sometimes one of the children is bitten or scratched by the dog, and even if the dog is playing, it can mean the dog is leaving the family.

We expect so much from our dogs and it is easy to forget they are dogs, not babysitters or supervisors, and they don't have a sense of what is right or wrong when it comes to children.

Introducing
Children to Dogs

Teach children how to pet your dog. Patting on the head is common but can be irritating to the dog. Instead, teach them to rub his shoulders, back, ribs, or belly if the dog will roll over to show his tummy. Teach them not to handle or force the dog to allow handling of tail, feet, ears, mouth, or eyes.

Dog Tales

George, a Rat Terrier, had been found in a trash heap, filthy, skinny, and covered with fleas. The couple who found him decided to keep him, so they started on the work of cleaning him up, getting him healthy, and eventually having him neutered. Housetraining was tricky, but they got it done.

George was about ten months old and turned out to a be bit feisty, barking at strangers and other dogs. The couple quickly found out he wasn't good with small children, growling and snarling at them. Around the same time, they found out they were expecting a baby themselves. Since they did not want to give up George, they basically divided their home to accommodate George's needs and allow for a child to grow up safely around him.

Strategic placement of baby gates, with George safely living in the lower level of the house, allowed him to spend time with the couple when the child was in bed. This worked out fine, and when the little boy was about three years old, George decided he was okay.

While the child and the dog still needed to be supervised, the family was able to incorporate George into the daily living schedule of the family.

Blending Dogs and Children *Continued*

Appropriate games for children and dogs

Let the dog get the toy sometimes to keep him in the game.

If at any time the dog chases the children instead of the toy, the game ends by teaching the children to "freeze" when the adult supervisor says to.

Children can help teach the dog to run through a tunnel. Always reward your dog with praise or a treat.

- **Hide-and-seek.** A child or children can carry a treat and go hide while the adult holds the dog and covers his eyes. When the dog is released and finds a child, he gets a treat. It's great for the child to ask the dog to sit before getting the treat, so the dog doesn't learn to jump on the kids.

- **Chase the toy.** An adult ties a squeaky or plush toy onto a six-foot cord or leash. The children take turns dragging the toy by the leash, while the dog chases the toy. Let the dog get the toy sometimes to keep him in the game. It's a good idea to have two or more of these toys ready if there are several children playing.

  If at any time the dog chases the children instead of the toy, the game ends by teaching the children to "freeze" when the adult supervisor says to. With all the children "frozen," the dog should go back to the toy, and the game can continue.

- **Retrieve.** If your dog retrieves a toy, having the children take a turn is great. If your dog just chases after the toy but doesn't return with it, have several toys available, always going to the next one to help the dog learn to bring his back.

- **Tricks.** If your dog knows several tricks, the children can each take a turn putting him through his paces. This is great because the dog learns to listen to everyone, even children, while getting lots of practice. Toy hoops, toy tunnels and even broom sticks work great for props, to teach the dog to hop through or over for a treat. The hoop can be placed on the ground and the dog gets a reward for being in the hoop.

Dog Tales

Teaching the dog a few simple tricks such as high-five and retrieve are fun for the dog and the children.

A dog that hurts children is in danger of losing his home and his life—even if it is determined the child or parent is at fault.

Dog owners must now be very proactive with anyone who wants to interact with the dog, even to the point of refusing if the dog is nervous, fearful, or uncomfortable.

Our first dog, Blossom, was a Rat Terrier. We were newly married and novices about raising a dog. We didn't even consider classes for her, and didn't have friends at that time with small children. So Blossom's first exposure to a toddler wasn't until Blossom was about a year old, and she was very frightened. She barked and growled and did her best to escape. You can imagine what she thought of this tiny human visitor that walked and fell down unpredictably and used those tiny hands to try to grab her ears.

It dawned on me she thought the toddler was dangerous. Blossom was only fifteen pounds and the toddler was big enough to put a scare into her. This was over 30 years ago, so the training then was to punish her for her aggressive behavior. I didn't punish her, I started giving her jobs (her series of ten or so tricks to perform). Soon she started accepting toddlers and figuring out that they carry and drop food everywhere. That helped.

In the sixteen years we had Blossom, we managed to do a lot of things wrong. We didn't socialize her to children or even strangers very well. While we didn't have any children ourselves, after I found out how afraid she was, I both trained and socialized her with children when I could. I did keep her close to me if there were small children around. She spent the last few years of her life entertaining hospital patients, doing tricks for the treats they would toss her.

Want to Trade

Q **Caller:** *Our dog Rover loves playing with the kids, and he never bites or threatens except when he has a rawhide bone. He loves these bones, so we want him to have them. What can we do to be sure he is safe around the children when he has a bone?*

A **Paula says:** *This is a time when I would recommend using a combination of training and management to keep everyone safe. For the management side, only offer Rover these valuable bones when there is no chance of his being disturbed by the children. It could be in his crate or a place where the children have been taught the dog is off limits. But even with these precautions, someone could make a mistake and dog, bone, and child could be in the same place.*

In addition to management, teach Rover to trade. Start with a bone or toy that Rover DOESN'T care about much, and use really good treats. Say something like: "Rover, do you want to TRADE?" using a happy tone of voice. Give him the treat. Then give him back the bone. Practice ten or so times then at the next session, use a better bone, and the same great treat. Always, he gets the treat and the bone back for giving up the bone.

When he willingly gives up his rawhides to the adults in the family, start teaching the same process to the kids (over seven years). They give him a treat and give the bone back each time.

Our goal is that if sometime a child reaches in to take his precious rawhide, Rover is going to think, "Yippee, where's my treat?". If and when it does happen, be sure to reward him.

Training a Dog
to TRADE:
A Young Dog's
First Lesson

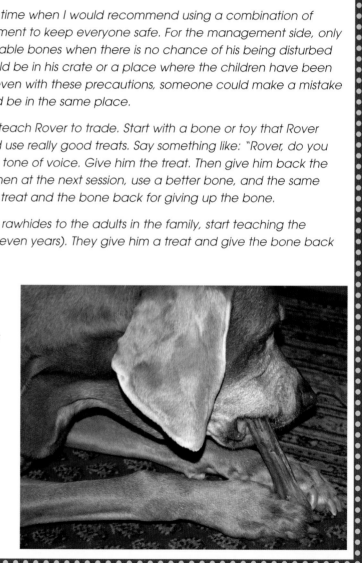

Jealousy

Q **Caller:** *We have a seven-year-old female Weimaraner. She has been very jealous, since our baby arrived. Our son is now 18 months old and the dog and baby are the greatest of friends. My concern is the dog, Abby, is very destructive and will tear things up the minute we aren't paying attention to her or if we try to confine her to a certain room or area of the house.*

We have had Abby since she was seven-and-a-half weeks old and up until recently she was the only 'baby'. It is hard to find time for walks now. We do have a fenced yard for her. We have another baby coming in July.

A **Paula says:** *We talk a lot about preparing the family dog for adding children to the family. Some of those techniques will help Abby even now, but her misbehaviors stem from her efforts to get attention. For example, if she is calmly lying on her bed nearby, most likely she is being ignored. But if she picks up a baby toy or clothing, barks, jumps or any unwanted behavior, she will get attention. The family will think they are stopping the behaviors by scolding or punishing her, when in reality they are teaching Abby how to get more attention.*

Start consciously rewarding Abby for good behaviors. Praise is nice, but treats or a short minute play session or massage can be much more rewarding. Dogs repeat behaviors that are rewarded, so it really helps to be aware of the behaviors you are rewarding.

Enrichment activities like a stuffed Kong®, playing tug for a few minutes, practicing tricks and scattering her meals in the grass can make a big difference for Abby. Perhaps a teenage friend could walk her. Or set up play dates with a compatible dog.

Follow up: *Abby was "put on the schedule" with this family. They acknowledged her needs and started meeting them as much as possible and it made a big difference in Abby's behavior.*

95

Topics:

Before You Begin

- Adult dogs can be housetrained in the same manner as puppies.
- Puppies have limited bladder control.
- Dogs and puppies like to be clean and to sleep in a clean area.
- All dogs do best when kept to a routine schedule.

Dog have to go potty

- When they wake up in the morning or after a nap.
- Shortly after eating and drinking.
- Before they go to sleep.
- After stressful events.
- After active play, and sometimes during it.
- If a dog, and especially a puppy, is not allowed to relieve himself at these times, he likely will have an accident.
- Be proactive. Don't wait for the dog to "tell" you he has to go out. Assume he does and take him outside.

Considering the Basics

Housetraining is critical and an immediate concern.

Any amount of time you spend on housetraining is time well spent.

The first few weeks of owning a puppy or dog are some of the hardest and the most important. Extra time and effort now will pay off in a big way.

Preventing Accidents

The goal of housetraining focuses on preventing accidents, instead of waiting for them to happen.

It is about making it easy for the puppy to do the right thing in the first place.

Training in this way takes a positive approach, and is faster and more effective than correcting for mistakes.

You play the most important role in the success or failure of this method, as you must be patient, determined, and consistent for it to work. If you already own an adult dog with housetraining problems, you can use this method to start fresh, just as you would for a puppy.

Puppy's First Night Home

When you first bring your puppy home, carry him from your car to the yard. Set him on the grass until he goes potty.

When he does, tell him how wonderful he is. Bring him inside and play with him so he feels comfortable in his new surroundings.

Take him outside at least every two hours while he is awake. Don't wait for him to make the first move.

Feed supper to the puppy in his crate. After that, carry him outside to potty before you do anything else. Wait for him to have a bowel movement before returning inside. Some pups handle this job quickly, while others take a half an hour to accomplish their task. Start using a word cue, such as "hurry up." Act happy when you have success. You must stay outside with the puppy. He won't understand what you are trying to teach him if you leave him outside alone.

It is important to always carry the puppy to the door and outside as soon as you open the crate. Puppies seem to have a reflex peeing action that clicks in the moment they step out of the crate onto your carpeting or wood floor. If you let him walk to the door, he will no doubt have an accident before he gets there. Part of this training is psychological. You want him to feel grass, not your floor, under his feet when he goes to the bathroom.

After another short play period, take the pup outside before bedtime, and then tuck him into his crate for the night. The crate should be placed near an adult bed so that if he cries during the night you can take him outdoors to potty. Carry him outside to potty and then put him back in the crate. If you play with him, he may decide it is play time, not sleep time.

Always carry the puppy to the door and outside as soon as you open the crate.

Take the pup outside before bedtime, and then tuck him into his crate for the night.

housetraining:
it's not rocket science

Daytime Schedule

● **Morning** - Immediately, carry the puppy outside to potty. Let him play inside for an hour in the room where you are.

● **Breakfast** - Feed the puppy in the crate, and don't let him out for about half an hour. Carry him outside to potty. A puppy usually has a bowel movement after each meal, so give him enough time to accomplish that task.

● **Play time** – Let the puppy play inside for an hour or so, but don't give him free run of the house. Use baby gates or closed doors to keep him out of rooms he should not explore. Puppies are notorious for turning out-of-the-way corners into bathrooms. If you give him too much freedom too soon, he will make a mistake.

● **After play time** - Take him outside and then tuck him into his crate for a nap. For the first month or so, you will be feeding three to four meals a day. Adult dogs only need two meals a day.

● **Repeat** - The same schedule should be repeated throughout the day. Play times can be lengthened as the puppy gets older and is more reliable. Eventually, the puppy will be letting you know when he needs to go out. Remember, if you ignore his request or don't move quickly, he will have an accident.

Creating a Daytime Schedule

Establish a regular schedule of puppy potty trips, play time, and feedings.

This helps you to control the times he goes out and helps prevent accidents in the house. These scheduling tips will help you get a routine in place:

We know this sounds like a lot of work, and honestly, it is. The results will pay off in a trained puppy and clean carpets. Some breeds are easier to housetrain than others.

A lot of your puppy's success will depend on how he was raised before he came to you. Pet store puppies allowed to use wire-bottom crates have less inclination to keep their crates clean. Puppies raised in barns or garages and allowed to "go" anywhere may be more difficult. Be patient. You can train them. It will just take a bit longer.

Consider using the umbilical method when the puppy has free time in the house. Use a soft buckle collar and leash that connect you to the puppy. This helps to prevent accidents, because you always know where the puppy is.

Ideally, you are reading this before you bring your new puppy or older dog home. But, if not, just pick up the schedule at an appropriate place for your situation.

Housetraining with a Crate

Housetraining and preventing accidents also calls for the use of a dog crate, or at least a small confined area for the pup to stay in when he can't be supervised. Think of the crate as your dog's private room, where he can rest and stay safe and secure, away from trouble. Your puppy needs to be protected from hurting himself, and from chewing your furniture. A crate will make the task much easier, but a small confined area will work.

In most cases, the crate will be more effective. You might want to block off part of the space in a larger crate while housetraining a puppy. You don't want the puppy to think he can potty in one end and sleep in the other, or, even worse, learn not to care if there is a mess. If you have purchased a crate for him to "grow into," use dividers to reduce the inner space while he is small.

An exercise pen and crate can help when you have to be gone longer than the puppy can hold it. The goal is the keep the crate clean, giving the puppy the opportunity to potty outside of it.

If your puppy must be left at home unsupervised, try using a different set up to help keep the puppy successfully pottying outside of the crate. You can use a very small room or a pen without a top called an exercise pen. These are plastic or wire, and can be folded up for storage. Place the exercise pen in a corner, using zip ties attached to poles to keep it straight and sturdy. Place the crate in one corner of the pen with the door removed or zip tied open. Place bedding and toys in the crate to make it cozy and inviting.

Cover the floor of the pen with papers or puppy pads to absorb accidents.

Water should be in sturdy bowl that won't tip easily. If you leave food for the puppy, make it a snack, not a meal. As soon as you get home, scoop the puppy up and take him outdoors to potty. Be sure to reward success outdoors! Never scold the puppy for messes in the pen. When you can leave him for short periods of time, close the door of the crate, gradually lengthening the time you leave him with the door closed. If the puppy messes in the pen while you are gone, you might have tried to leave him too long. Change the papers several times a day if they have been soiled.

Commit to a routine of taking your dog outdoors immediately when you get home. Even if he was only in the crate for ten minutes, open the door and take him outside to potty. He will learn to try to wait until you get home to go potty.

Refer to Crate Training in Chapter 8 for information on crate training basics.

Make the crate comfortable for the puppy by adding a sleeping pad and toys. Place the crate in an area the family spends time so your puppy won't feel isolated.

Paper Training or Potty Pads?

By only allowing the puppy to relieve himself outside, you are reinforcing the idea it is not acceptable to do it inside.

Using newspapers and potty pads in the house will confuse the puppy.

Many puppies also get the idea that going potty near the papers is as good as going on them. If it is necessary to use newspapers when you are gone, be sure to keep to the regular housetraining schedule when you are home. Get the puppy outside often and do not leave the papers out "just in case."

Keeping Your Dog's Yard Clean

Keep your dog's yard clean and free of old stools.

Many dogs choose a favorite area to use as a bathroom.

If that space becomes dirty, the inside of the house may start to look attractive, and you do not want to take that chance. If your dog is tied up when he is outside to potty, it is even more crucial to keep the area clean. Picking up also gives you insight into your pet's health. Stools should be firm and well formed. Loose ones can be an indication of health problems, such as worms, stress, or digestive upset.

Accidents

Possible Reasons for Accidents:

Feeding issues, changes in diet, health problems and emotional upsets (a new pet or a new family member) can cause your puppy or dog to have accidents.

Feeding: Almost all dog food bags suggest feeding guidelines. Your pet might need less food than suggested. Puppies often eat more than they need, because they like the taste of the food. If your puppy is having more than three or four stools a day, try cutting back the food a little and using a measuring cup to feed consistent portions. Your veterinarian can help you monitor the pup's growth and condition.

Consider feeding an optimal food. If the first few ingredients listed are mostly grain, such as corn, oats, or rice, you might consider changing to a food with meat ingredients such as chicken, in the first three listings. Meal means meat that has been ground and dried; generally, it is a good product. If meat by-products are listed, these can be nearly anything left in the rendering process and are not necessarily beneficial as an ingredient. Find what works best for your dog.

Changes in dog food brands or overindulging in treats or table scraps can cause diarrhea. If you do change brands, do it gradually by mixing old and new food for several days. A change in water supply can cause problems, too. If you are moving or traveling, take along a couple gallons of "home" water to mix with the new.

Accidents *Continued*

Health problems: Diabetes in adult dogs and urinary tract infections in both dogs and puppies are common and can cause frequent urination. Such infections are common in female puppies. A symptom is frequent or unpredictable squatting with little urine release. If you suspect a physical problem, check with your veterinarian.

Freedom: Another problem we find with pet owners frustrated with housetraining is that they give the puppy or dog too much freedom. Keeping a leash on the dog in the house can make the difference between an accident and a successful trip to the door.

Dirty conditions: Housetraining dogs from dirty or abusive housing situations can be tough. Dogs raised in filth or on wire, such as puppy mill dogs, get used to living in messes, so it takes time to adapt to a clean environment. When housetraining dogs from such situations, you need to arm yourself with patience, supervision, and effort.

Troubleshooting

Puppies, especially those under three months old, have limited bladder control and reflexes. They can't predict they need to "go" until the critical moment. Therefore, it is not realistic to expect them to let you know ahead of time. If you are observant you will notice that a puppy looking for a place to go potty will circle about while sniffing the floor. The sniffing is instinctive—he is looking for a place that has already been used. If he can't find one, he'll start one. By preventing accidents inside, you'll teach him that the only appropriate bathroom is outside.

Preventing Accidents

This method of housetraining your dog or puppy using a crate and paying attention to schedules, feeding and freedom is based on preventing accidents.

If you are diligent in taking your dog outside often enough, you will get fast results.

If your puppy makes a mistake because you did not get him out when you should have, it is not really his fault.

If you catch the pup in the act, stay calm. Make a startling noise, such as clapping your hands, to try to stop the action. Carry him outside to an area he has already used. As you set him on the ground, tell him, "Go potty." Praise him if he finishes the job.

Keeping a leash on the dog in the house can make the **difference between an accident and a successful trip to the door.**

Accidents *Continued*

Cleaning Up Accidents

Potty accidents will invariably happen with puppies. If there is an accident, put your puppy or adult dog out of sight while you clean up a puddle. Cleaning a vinyl floor is fairly simple. For carpeting, get lots of paper towels, and blot with fresh paper towels until you have lifted as much liquid as possible.

Don't use a cleaner with ammonia, as that will attract the puppy or dog back to the scene of the accident. In a pinch, dilute white vinegar 1:1 with water. Pick a product from your veterinarian or pet store, that will neutralize the ammonia, not just mask the odor.

Dogs are attracted to urine odors and their noses are better than ours. They can pick up even a tiny residue from a commercial odor-killer. Watch that spot in the future.

Troubleshooting

What if your dog goes potty while you are gone?

Try one or more of these options:

- Change his feeding schedule.

- Do a "double potty" trip outdoors before you leave him.

- If he goes potty because of anxiety, talk to a dog behavior expert about options.

- Check out doggy daycare.

- Ask a friend or neighbor to come in during the day for a walk or potty time.

Choose a cleaning product that will neutralize the accident's ammonia odor or your dog will keep revisiting that same spot.

Housetraining Older Dogs

If you are trying to train an older dog or one that is having housetraining problems, start from the beginning with a modified puppy schedule.

Use a crate and put your dog on a schedule.

An older dog can be expected to control himself for longer periods if you take him outside at critical times—first thing in the morning, after meals, and the last thing at night. Get him outside every three to four hours between those times.

Adopted older dogs that have become used to the freedom to potty off leash outdoors might not have a bowel movement when on a leash. Walk them a little longer, use a long line or a flexi-lead, or keep them confined until they really have to go. You don't want your dog to practice making mistakes in your house. More freedom in the house comes with more reliability.

Make sure he is done before taking him back indoors. The process is a little trickier with an adult dog. Instead of plucking him up to take outside, use a leash and be sure to take him out more often.

Use a crate and modified puppy schedule to housetrain older dogs.

Have Your Dog Checked by a Veterinarian

Housetraining my own ARL adopted Chow pup Fox became most frustrating when she stopped and urinated in front of me, without any of the usual signals that dogs give. There was no sniffing, standing still, turning in a circle, or moving toward the door. She would be walking along, stop, and pee.

Fortunately, I thought to have her urine checked by a veterinarian. Sure enough, she had a urinary tract infection. Infections, crystals in the urine, or other medical issues can complicate our training efforts. Sometimes your dog simply can't make it outdoors, even to the point of no control. With Fox, it took two rounds of antibiotics to clear it up. After the discomfort was gone, she was more than willing to get outdoors in time to potty.

Keep in mind that if you are having housetraining issues, it might be wise to ask your veterinarian to check urine and stools for medical issues. Once they are cleared up, many dogs housetrain quickly.

Topics:

Basic Training and Cues

In this section you will learn how training your dog self-control and manners using the "Nothing In Life Is Free" system can make everyday living with your dog enjoyable for both of you.

Your dog will learn to:

- Sit quietly while you put on his leash.
- Stay and wait for permission to go through any door.
- Sit politely to be petted by friends in your home or by strangers on the street.
- Give up something he has stolen because you have taught him to trade.
- Back away from something dangerous on the floor or the sidewalk because you have taught him to leave it.

We encourage you to start training as soon as you get your dog. Enroll him in classes. Keep working with and training him. You will soon discover there are many wonderful things your dog can learn.

The Importance of Consistency

Consistency among family members is key when training your dog. To avoid confusing the dog and frustrating the family, we encourage all family members to use similar voice tones, body language, and the same words and gestures when training him.

"Nothing in Life is Free" Training System

We have been teaching the "Nothing In Life Is Free" system for many years. It is the foundation for all of our training. In brief, the dog learns that when he behaves the way we want him to behave, he will always be rewarded for the desired behavior. For example, your dog learns that Sit gets a favorite treat. If your dog wants to go for a walk, he knows he has to sit quietly while his leash is put on. He knows that if he jumps, squirms or does anything but Sit, you will put the leash away. You may return and try again in a few minutes, but, if the dog does not immediately perform the desired behavior you've requested, he must wait for his walk.

The "Nothing In Life is Free" system is not a magic pill that will solve a specific behavior problem. Rather, it is a way of living with your dog that will help him behave better. He trusts and accepts you as his leader, is confident knowing his rules and boundaries in your family. He learns that when he behaves, he receives a positive reward.

Training Self-Control

One of the first things to train any puppy is self-control. You may have seen puppies that move randomly and frantically, chew anything in reach, or bark and whine to get attention. Puppies may even resort to growling or snarling— behaviors often associated with food, bone or toy guarding, or they may nip when handled or restrained.

At the shelter we see many teenage dogs (four to eighteen months) with handling issues. They have learned that frantic jumping and running can get them a chase game, that a growl or snap will get them released or that grabbing toys and shoes garners attention. When that attention is scolding it may not be the attention the puppy wants, but it IS attention. Without proper training, inappropriate behaviors continue and become more and more challenging to correct. It is so easy for an owner to react. If every time the dog whines the owner responds by asking him why he is upset, the dog quickly learns whining gets attention. This can lead to a very whiney dog. If you've allowed your cute, small puppy to jump up for attention, when that same puppy is a 50-pound adolescent, jumping up is no longer cute. We encourage you to take every opportunity to reward good behavior early and build on that to train the dog self-control. Here's how to start.

"Nothing In Life is Free"

Summary

Always use positive reinforcement to train your dog self-control

- Teach your dog a few cues and/or tricks.

- Practice.

- Before giving your dog a reward he must perform the desired behavior when you cue him.

A young puppy quickly learns that Sit gets a treat. Start training as soon as you get your dog.

1 Hold the food bowl just over your dog's head so he's watching it.

2 Using the food bowl, cue your dog to sit by <u>slowly</u> moving the food bowl over his forehead.

3 When the dog is sitting, lower the food bowl.

4 Put the bowl down and let him eat.

Teaching a Child the Correct Way to Feed a Puppy

Training Self-Control *Continued*

Training – Session 1

Training "Nothing In Life Is Free" at mealtime

Begin right away with the food bowl to start training a dog or puppy self-control.

People often leave the food bowl out, allowing the dog or puppy to eat whenever he wants. This can complicate housetraining efforts, as well as give the dog the idea that food is free and has no strings attached to humans. It can also make using treats for training much less effective. So, we suggest you begin training using the food bowl as a teaching tool.

Put food in the food bowl as usual and get your dog's attention. If your dog knows the cue for Sit, you use it, just once to help him understand what the game is about. If he doesn't yet know a Sit cue, stand patiently holding the food bowl over his head until he stops jumping up, running around or another similar behavior and quiets down.

In this instance, the food bowl is being used as both the cue and the lure (reward) for your dog to Sit. Cue your dog to Sit by slowly moving the food bowl back over his forehead. He should be watching the food bowl. Cue the dog to Sit just once. When the dog sits, put down the food bowl. Refer to Training Sit on page 108.

If after a few minutes of your standing patiently holding the food bowl, your dog hasn't yet sat down, put the food bowl away and repeat again later, waiting until he is sitting before lowering the bowl to feed him.

"Nothing In Life Is Free"

You can teach this self-control behavior based on "Nothing In Life Is Free" in other areas of your dog's life, such as petting, leash walks, picking up keys to the car, going in and out of doors and any other time that you would prefer him to sit instead of demand.

Training – Session 2

At the next session, same scenario, cue Sit one time only, and then stand there with the bowl waiting for the SIT. When your dog does sit and you start to lower the bowl, he will likely stand or jump up. Stand straight back up with the bowl, without saying a word, and wait for the dog to sit again. Chances are, he will sit much quicker this time but it could still take a few minutes.

Waiting while your dog figures out on his own how to get you to lower the food bowl is worth the patience it takes on your part. Over the next few meals, he will start to anticipate your lowering the bowl and will stay calm or sit before you ask. If he doesn't or forgets, just stand still and let him think about it. Dogs learn so much better when we let them figure out how to do what we want, which to them is all about getting what they want.

Training – Session 3

To advance this to the next level, your dog not only has to sit while you lower the bowl, he needs to stay sitting until you release him to come eat. For this, you will need the Sit cue and a release word. Most people use "OK." You use the same process as in the previous sessions, but this time, If he sits and then stands or jumps forward to eat, you pick the bowl back up. Each time he raises his rear to get up before you say "OK," you will pick up the bowl. Quickly, he will learn that sitting and staying in that sit until he hears "OK," gets him his meal.

Please, resist the temptation to take back the bowl after you have said "OK" and released your dog to eat. This will seem like teasing to the dog and may cause him to start guarding the bowl from you, even to the point of threatening you. At the very least, it could cause him to hurry to eat his meal, which may not be healthy. Once you've released the dog to eat, let him eat.

Begin Training Good Manners with the Food Bowl

Get your dog used to you handling her food bowl by hand-feeding her a few pieces of food from the bowl. Here, six-month-old Bella is learning to Sit and is enjoying being hand-fed.

Defining the terms

- **Lure:** the treat

- **Cue Hand:** the hand that gives the hand signals

- **Lure/Cue Hand:** the treat is in the hand giving the hand signals

- **Lure Hand:** holds the treats (lures)

- **Jackpots:** Many trainers use jackpots, five or more treats at one time to reward the dog when he does especially well. For example, if you are working on Sit and he immediately sits the first time you use a verbal cue without a hand signal, give him several of his favorite treats. He will remember what he did to get those treats and work to repeat that behavior.

  Some trainers dispense the treats one at a time in succession and others reward with all five at once. Determine what works best for your dog. Don't give too many jackpots or they are no longer special.

Training Sit Using Cue/Lure and Reward

Sit Goal: Dog sits quietly with her tail and hindquarters on the floor.

There are 3 progress levels when training Sit.

Level 1: Luring the Sit behavior and giving the lure as a reward.

Level 2: Sit with hand signal (cue) but reward comes from somewhere else.

Level 3: Adding a Verbal Cue and Proofing the Behavior with Distractions.

Beautiful Nettie spent her early years in a cramped puppy mill cage having litter after litter of puppies. She was rescued by ARL-Iowa and adopted. Today, she visits the sick and elderly and is loved by everyone.

Level 1: Luring the Sit behavior and giving the lure as a reward

At Level 1, a hand over the dog's head means SIT. You use only the lure/cue hand to signal and treat. Do not say Sit or say your dog's name, just reward her with the treat and offer praise each time she follows the cue. Use quiet, calm praise, because you don't want her to get excited and stand up when she is sitting. Resist the urge to say Sit even if your dog already knows the verbal cue for Sit. You are training a technique as well as a behavior and once the "cue/lure/reward" technique is understood, you can teach her many behaviors using just this method. But in the beginning, we want to be silent until we are sure the dog understands a hand over her head means Sit.

Have ten or so treats per session ready in a bag, bowl, or your pocket. Keep two or three in your lure/cue hand so you can quickly deliver them to your dog. Also remember to praise your dog each time she is successful. The rest of the time, you are silent.

Practice this behavior at least three times in sets of ten. Count out ten treats, use them as a set, and repeat just a few times.

If you start to get frustrated and need to take a break, toss a treat to the side of the dog for her to get it "for free" and restart later. One of the amazing things about dogs is even when you are sure they don't get grasp what you are trying to teach, they often understand it quickly when you start over.

Defining the terms

● **Treats:** When training dogs, work with soft, tasty treats that are easy to carry and count out. You want to be able to do many repetitions and keep the dog's interest at the same time. You may need to have a mixture of several of your dog's favorite treats handy.

Commercial treats can be used, but also try Cheerios and other low-sugar cereals, cubes of cheese, or fat-free turkey hot dogs cut into very small pieces. Stay away from high-salt and high-sugar treats. Consider cutting up treats and putting them in plastic bags to freeze, so you can grab a few bags to be thawed by the time you need them.

Try different treat options to see what your dog likes. Have several treats for training, but save his favorites for his best efforts and for jackpots.

Training SIT

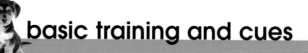
Training Sit Using Cue/Lure and Reward *Continued*

Level 1: Sit—Large Dog

1 Start by standing upright with your dog on a leash. Have treats ready.

2 Hold the treat in your lure/cue hand just over the dog's nose, eyebrow or forehead.

3 When the dog makes the slightest effort to drop her hindquarters, give her the treat and praise. Watch her back towards her tail, not her head.

If she sits right away, give her the treat and continue to give her all ten treats, one each second, unless she stands up.

Note: Giving several treats is the start of Stay behavior and teaches her that staying in a Sit position will be rewarded.

Level 1: Sit—Small Dog

1 Start by standing upright with your dog on a leash. Hold the treat in your lure/cue hand just over the dog's nose, eyebrow or forehead.

Note: Sometimes, bending over can be intimidating to a small dog. If this is the case with your dog, kneel to teach Sit.

2 When the dog makes the slightest effort to drop her hindquarters, give her the treat and praise. Watch her back towards her tail, not her head.

3 If she sits right away, give her the treat and continue to give her all ten treats, one each second, unless she stands up.

Note: This is the start of Stay behavior and teaches her that staying in a Sit position will be rewarded.

Training a
Puppy to SIT

Training Sit Using Cue/Lure and Reward *Continued*

Troubleshooting:

If your dog has figured out the treat is not in your Cue Hand and won't Sit, there is an intermediate level to help with the changeover.

- Start with a treat in each hand, using your Lure/Cue Hand as in level 1, but when the dog performs she doesn't get a treat from the Lure/Cue Hand. Instead, you reach to get the treat from your other hand. Your dog will learn the treat comes anyway but with a tiny delay. If you practice this step a few times, you will be able to go on to the next step without the treat in your Lure/Cue hand.

- If you are having trouble getting the desired behavior, contact a trainer for help.

Level 2: Sit with hand signal (cue) but reward comes from somewhere else

In Level 1 the treat is in the Lure/Cue Hand. Now you are going to have the treat in your other hand, a pocket or on a nearby counter. Don't rush to this level, but don't avoid it either. When your dog is sitting readily at least four out of five times or 80 percent (when you Lure/Cue with one hand) start putting the treat in your other hand. Now you are cuing the dog with the Cue Hand and getting the treats from the Lure Hand. You give treats with each correct result, but they come a bit slower, because you have to reach to get the treat. Deliver the treat right to her mouth, so she doesn't have to get up or move to get it. That helps keep her in the sitting position.

You should be ready to start this level after just a few sessions of Level 1 with your dog. Use the same pattern of three sets of ten treats. Practice whenever you get a chance, ideally two or three times a day, but only a minute or two each time.

Be sure to verbally praise your dog as well as reward her. Eventually you want your dog to work for your praise, as well as the occasional treat. Pairing praise with food increases the value of the praise and helps the dog understand she can enjoy a reward of praise only. This will help you during the many times you will ask her to do something when you don't have treats with you and praise is the reward.

If your dog starts to jump up instead of sit, you may be holding the treat too high over his head. Try keeping it closer to him. Each dog has a different target point that will work best.

Some dogs do best if the treat is close to the target spot, and some do better if the treat is held a few inches above it.

If he stands up, back up a step, encourage him to come to you and start over. Backing up a step gives him a chance to stand in front of you again and allows you to reset the exercise.

Level 3: Adding a Verbal Cue and Proofing the Behavior

Now that your dog will quickly and willingly sit with a hand signal, it is time to add a verbal cue. Pick the word or phrase you want to use. Everyone in the household should use the same one. I mention phrase, because while dog trainers tend to use one word cues, most families use phrases such as "Sit down", "Lie down."

1. Start with your ten treats in a treat bag or bowl nearby. Say your cue word or phrase and use your Cue Hand signal one second after you say the cue. Your dog might look at you questioningly for a second or two, but resist the urge to repeat either the hand signal or verbal cue. Just stand there and see what the dog does.

2. The first few times she might hesitate to sit but if she seems to be going to sit, reward her for her try. After that, wait a few seconds after you have cued her and let her do the sit before rewarding her. Adding the verbal cue might be confusing at first so help her work through the change.

3. Continue to work through your set of ten and then give her a rest.

Proofing the Behavior

To "proof" the behavior means we practice with distractions, such as people, other pets, or in different locations and at different times of day. You also want to start varying your body positions to help the dog learn whether you are sitting down, standing up, looking at her or turning away, if you say or cue Sit to her, it always means the same thing and will always be rewarded with praise and treats.

Start by moving the training with your dog across the room. While it seems simple to us, this one change can alter a dog's perception of the training. You may have to revert to a treat in the Lure/Cue hand for a few trials. Don't worry you will quickly be able to progress back to the verbal cue.

Repeated Verbal Cues

If you repeat the verbal cue, you will lose the effect of getting the dog to respond quickly.

Repeated cues can become "white noise" and easy for the dog to ignore.

It is also easy to start sounding more stern and gruff with each repetition. You want to keep the verbal cues soft, quiet and interesting.

Training Sit Using Cue/Lure and Reward *Continued*

Practice three sets of ten treats with her. Move out to the garage and do more. This training can be tough mental work for your dog. It seems to be as tiring for dogs as a good run or play session. Teaching new behaviors, including tricks, can be used when you and your dog can't get outside for your regular exercise.

Note: Your dog does not need to be on a leash in the house, as she should be eager to stay and interact. However when you move outdoors, keep her safe on a leash or in a fenced area. It may take six or more moves for your dog to start to understand that the location is not important and she can perform the behavior anywhere and get the same rewards from you. This is called generalization. The more you change locations and add distractions to your training, the stronger the cues and results will become.

Training Lie Down

Very often owners have taught Sit to their dog but are stuck on trying to teach a Lie Down or Drop behavior. Lie Down is a tougher behavior to get dogs to do for us. To teach this behavior, we will follow the same pattern we used for Sit.

Goal: Dog lies down quietly with her body on the floor.

As with Sit, there are 3 progress levels when training Lie Down

Level 1: Luring the Lie Down behavior and giving an immediate reward.

Level 2: Using the hand signal to get the Lie Down behavior and giving the treat from your other hand.

Level 3: Adding a Verbal Cue and Proofing the Behavior with Distractions.

Note: Whether your dog is large or small, the process is the same with the exception that we recommend you kneel for a small dog and stand for a large dog.

Keeping Track

Using ten treats at a time is a simple way to keep track of when to move on with your training.

If your dog performs eight times out of ten, move on to the next step or level.

If not, stay at the same level until your dog can get at least eight out of ten right. This will be used with all the behaviors we train.

Training an
Older Dog to
LIE DOWN or DROP

Level 1: Luring the Behavior—Small Dog

To make this simpler for you and your dog, we reward the dog's incremental or tiny bits of effort.

1 Start with your dog sitting. Don't forget to continue to reward the Sit behavior. Using your Lure/Cue Hand, take the treat and show it to the dog. Slowly drop your hand to the floor keeping the treat in front of the dog.

2 Usually her nose will follow your hand with the treat. Her shoulders will start to move, and her elbows will drop even if it is just a little bit. If the dog lowers her body at all, slip her the treat and praise. Each time you lure her toward the floor, wait just a little bit longer as she lowers to the floor to give the treat.

3 Most dogs will lie down in two to four tries, because it is easier to get the treat and the crouching position can get uncomfortable.

4 For some dogs, you may work the dog under your bent knee (or under the rungs of a chair).

Under the knee option (see Step 4). Using your Lure/Cue hand, encourage your dog to follow it under your knee. Your goal, and the behavior you want to reward, is the dog lowering her shoulders to prepare to crouch. If your dog will lower her shoulders to follow the treat under your knee, reward her with a treat three or four times, and then try it without using your bent knee. You can also use this technique with large dogs since the goal is not to get the dog under your knee but rather to get the dog into a crouch position so you can reward her. If you are still having trouble with this behavior, move on to another and come back to it.

Training Lie Down *Continued*

Troubleshooting:

If you have tried over and over and your dog just won't lie down, look for reasons she may be reluctant.

Maybe the floor is slippery or uncomfortable, or there are distractions in the room.

- Try varying the placement of your hand as you lower the treat.

- Try faster, slower, farther ahead of the dog, or closer to the dog. One of these positions should start to work.

If you have a small dog you might want to work on a low table or a bottom stair step. This will enable you to put the treat below the level of the "floor" and encourage your dog to lie down. If you get a "shoulders down" but "tail in the air" position, reward it once. During the next try, wait to reward a full lie-down position.

Training a Puppy to
LIE DOWN or DROP

Level 2: Using the hand signal to get the Lie Down behavior and giving the treat from your other hand

You have been practicing using a Lure/Cue to get your dog to lie down and are probably taking the treat straight to the floor.

1. Now, hold one treat in your Cue/Lure hand and put 10 treats in your other hand, the Lure hand.

2. Give the same Cue signal as in Level 1, the treat in your Lure/Cue hand and leading your dog into a Lie Down position. Using your Lure/Cue hand, reach to your other hand and pick a treat. Quickly give the treat directly to your dog, hopefully before she gets up. If she does get up, try to give her the treat as close to the floor as possible.

3. When your dog is successfully following your Lure/Cue hand with the treat you have been holding, give her the same cue without the treat. You will need to be quick about getting the treat from your other hand, pocket or counter (Lure Hand). You are building trust with the dog as she begins to understand the treat will still be there, even though it may be delayed a few seconds and coming from another location.

    When you are able to Cue your dog to Lie Down without a treat in your Cue hand, start to minimize the downward motion of the Cue hand signal. Our goal is to be able to give the hand Cue for Lie Down from a standing position without having to bend over as we do in Level 1 when we take the treat to the floor. You will know if you are going too fast or if your dog doesn't understand when she sits instead of lies down or if she keeps looking away. When you can depend on your dog to lie down at least eight out of ten times when you give her the signal, you are ready to move on.

Level 3: Adding a Verbal Cue and Proofing the Behavior with distractions

Now that you can give a hand signal to your dog while standing in front of her and she will lie down, it is time to add the verbal cue. If you aren't to this point, practice a bit more or seek a coach to help you and your dog.

1. Say the verbal cue and then give your hand signal. Your dog might be a bit confused the first few times, so be patient and wait for her to figure it out. Do not repeat verbal cues or hand signals more than once. If the dog is still confused, practice the hand signal a few more times and reward her for success, before adding the verbal cue.

2. When the dog is comfortable with both signals, try just saying the verbal cue. Again, say it once. Don't repeat it, just wait. If your dog hesitantly guesses and is right, that is a good time for a special treat or a jackpot.

Proofing the Behavior

Begin to practice your verbal cues with distractions. Start with easy ones, such as turning on the TV or moving to a different room. Be patient and work through this stage carefully. If your dog falters, chances are you have added too much too fast. Go back to the place where your dog has been successful to restart the training.

If your dog remains lying down when you add distractions, this is a good time for special treats.

Dog Tales

I had one ingenious student teach her Greyhound to lie down by rewarding her for it in her crate. She couldn't find a way to reward her any other place, but the dog always would lie down in her crate. So starting with success and really good treats there, she could get her to start lying down in other spots. It is fairly typical of retired racing Greyhounds to be reluctant to lie down. They learn to sit, but are more muscled in their hindquarters than most dogs and usually sit on their own muscles instead of the bones of their hip. They are never encouraged to sit or lie down in their training for the track, so it takes patience and creativity to get the behavior from these special dogs.

Watch the DVD to see how to train LIE DOWN

with an untrained dog and puppy awaiting adoption.

Training a LIE DOWN or DROP with a Hand Signal and Verbal Cue

Several short sessions will work better than trying to work for an hour. As with other exercises if your dog is frustrated or bored, he will let you know by turning or walking away. Ask for a Sit or another successful and easy behavior and end your session. Try again after a little while.

During the whole Stay training program, go back to your dog to reward him. It is tempting to call him to you from a Stay position, but it is best to train Come as a separate exercise. This way your dog doesn't start to anticipate the option to Come and move out of a Stay.

Many trainers and some owners use treat bags, but some dogs become focused on the treat bag instead of concentrating on their owner.

If you can be less predictable about where the treat comes from, the dog will tend to focus on you.

Training Stay Using Cue/Lure and Reward

Goal: Dog remains in one spot until given an end signal.

Stay means the dog doesn't move from that spot until you give him the end signal. The end signal can be any word. Common ones are "done," "over," or "OK." When training Stay, use treats to reward the dog while he stays and also after the end signal word is given. So, treat, treat, treat, while the dog stays. Then give the end signal to release the dog and treat. It seems like a lot of treats at the beginning, but it helps the dog to learn the difference between doing the behavior and ending the behavior. When teaching Stay the treats are always hidden in your pocket, treat bag, or hand.

There are 3 progress levels when training Stay.

Level 1: Getting the Stay behavior, giving an immediate reward and Proofing the Behavior with Simple Distractions

Level 2: Adding the Hand Signal

Level 3: Adding the Verbal Cue

Training STAY and RECALL

You can teach Stay in a Sit or Lie Down position.

Some happy endings
from the Animal Rescue League of Iowa

Bree

I'm a great fan of Border Collies so in Spring 2003, when ARL called me about a six-week old litter of Border Collie pups, I was happy to help.

I visited them every day, watched them play, bathed them and held them. Together with a friend from Border Collie Rescue of Minnesota we evaluated the litter to decide which would make great pets and which would need a job to keep them out of trouble.

We also evaluated them for agility. We agreed that the pick of the litter was one with a beautiful white blaze on her nose who was a great retriever, fast and gorgeous. The one with the less-classic black face and soft brown eyes was not as quick to retrieve, but did hold her own.

I wasn't certain I wanted another dog, but I remember walking by the kennel where the litter was kept. All the puppies would be sleeping except the one with the soft brown eyes and black face. She always seemed to know I was there and would gently lift her head to look at me.

My friend took the litter to Minnesota for adoption, but kept the one with the black face and soft brown eyes to foster. Seven years ago I adopted that puppy, Cool Breeze—Bree for short—and I've never regretted it. We've become a great team. She learned to play agility and was the 2009 Open National winner at the North American Dog Agility Council Championships.

I am often asked how I picked such a wonderful dog.

Well—it was the way she looked at me.

Suzanne

Raven

Raven came to the ARL as a stray when she was just about 4 months of age. After years of Stephen and I both working at the ARL we had never adopted our own dog due to the fact we rented. We finally bought our own house and when Raven came in I knew I had to foster her. She was so beautiful. Stephen had a love for dobies and we had a few come in but we just didn't feel the connection. Stephen was not working that day and I definitely wanted to foster her so I took her home and stood on the deck with her and called for her new daddy. After several minutes of excuses why she couldn't stay and after squashing those excuses, he couldn't resist her and said to bring her on in. She is now almost 4-1/2 years of age. Raven is a tennis ball freak and always needs to have two in her mouth. She loves to run and chase tennis balls but is reluctant to give them back. The backyard is always full of yellow tennis balls. She also enjoys her chewies and stuffed animals. Raven lives with her feline friends and is an attention seeker. She is a sweet girl who loves getting her way.

Terri and Steve

Agility Demonstration

Training Stay Using Cue/Lure and Reward *Continued*

Level 1: Getting the Stay behavior, giving an immediate reward and Proofing the behavior with simple distractions

Training Stay in a Sit or Lie Down position is the same. Practice with both positions. Several techniques will work, so see which you like best for your dog.

1 Have a handful of treats and ask for a Sit. Here, Robin hides the treats in her hand.

2 As long as your dog stays in the SIT, deliver one treat at a time approximately one second apart, right to his mouth about ten times. Say the end signal, let him get up and immediately "treat." At this point your dog doesn't know the behavior. You are standing in front of your dog delivering treats as long as he stays put. Deliver the treats to his mouth. Do not call him to come to you for the treat or you are training him to move out of Stay.

3 If your dog gets up and walks away, bring him back to the starting point and cue Sit. Follow the Stay procedure treat, treat, treat. Chances are your dog is sticking with you enjoying the 'free' treats.

4 At the next session, start with the same procedure but add a small step to one side or the other before treating. Start very small. Treat while he stays. If your dog starts to come with you, stop the treats. Don't scold or frown at him, simply start over. Usually after two or three trials, your dog will figure out if he stays put he will get treats. He will begin to stay while you move. After delivering ten treats, say your end signal and walk a few steps away. You dog can't make a mistake when you say O. K. and he leaves the Stay. Deliver a treat.

Paula Says

I sometimes use a "done" hand signal with both empty hands held up, palms toward the dog.

He quickly learns no treats are available and we are done working.

Training Stay Using Cue/Lure and Reward *Continued*

Level 2: Adding the Hand Signal

In Level 1, your dog learned if he stays in one spot while you step to the side, he will get a treat. Now, you want to add a hand signal and teach him to Stay for a span of time.

The hand signal for Stay is generally a vertical hand with fingers up and the palm toward the dog, much like a "stop" signal.

After you are able to move sideways several steps, try walking around your dog. Add the hand signal. Treat. This can be difficult for your dog and he may crane his neck to try to watch you. Keep a treat in front of his nose as you circle around him. He will learn that when you come back to face him, that is when he will get another treat.

Some dogs understand Stay quickly while others don't understand why they should stay still while you move. Keep practicing and when your dog is doing well in one location, move to another one to see if the behavior has been learned.

Level 3: Adding a Verbal Cue and more distractions

After your dog has learned the hand signal, add the verbal Stay.

As before say the new verbal signal before using your hand signal. Proof Stay by using it for short times on your walks, in stores, and around the house. Be sure to reward your dog after the end signal is given.

Ask for a Stay and add the Hand Signal for any position your dog is in, usually a Sit or Lie Down.

Training STAY with a Hand Signal and Verbal Cue

Training Your Dog to Come When You Call

Goal: Dog will Come to you when one word is given.

Training your dog to come to you is a basic command with many training options. This is the method we have found most successful.

There are 3 progress levels when training Come.

Level 1: Getting the Come behavior using the cue word and giving an immediate reward.

Level 2: Getting the Come behavior while moving around the room and cueing back and forth with another person.

Level 3: Proofing the Behavior.

Decide on the cue word or phrase you want to say when you call your dog. We suggest using the dog's name and the cue word, Come. Say the dog's name to get her attention. She looks at you for the next instruction. It will be Come.

So, we are training the dog two things.

1. Look at me when I say your name.

2. Come to me when I say the cue word, Come.

Because the dog's name becomes very important in this exercise, you should be careful how and when you say her name. You want her to associate her name with things she enjoys, like walks or dinner time.

Don't call her to come to you when you want to perform a task she doesn't like, such as getting her nails clipped.

Just go get her, use a leash to get her to come with you, and don't use her name.

Get your dog's attention by calling her name and saying Come.

Training Your Dog To Come When You Call *Continued*

Level 1: Getting the Behavior

Say your dog's name. When she looks at you, preferably making eye contact, present her with one piece of food directly to her mouth. You should be close to your dog. Add your cue word, Come, to her name early in this exercise since she will be responding quickly.

Be close to your dog when you begin so you can deliver the treat right after you say Come

Level 2:

Repeat Step 1 with ten to twenty pieces of food, moving around the room, if necessary, to keep your dog returning to you. If someone else is available, split the food, and call your dog back and forth. Each time she comes, she gets one piece of food. The more people, the merrier and quicker the exercise goes. Plus we are building lots of practice into this exercise. A round robin game of "Nettie, Come" can get a quick response in just a few practices.

With another person, call your dog back and forth using your dog's name, the cue word Come and plenty of treats.

Level 3: Proofing the Behavior

Begin to expect your dog to Come, as well as Sit politely before presenting the food. Resist saying Sit, instead wait for her to guess. If she jumps up or wanders off, use her name again to get her attention. She will quickly learn Come and Sit gets treats.

You want your dog to be consistent with this exercise so when you take it outdoors and add distractions, she will still respond quickly.

When you do take this exercise outside, it is important to use really wonderful treats instead of dog food. Escalating the quality of the treat keeps her on task when there are distractions. You will want to keep her on a leash when working outside so she doesn't wander off. You may want to purchase a long line, which has a leash-like clip but is fifteen or more feet long. You can also get a thin cord from the hardware store and purchase a leash clip to tie on one end.

Training a Dog to
COME when CALLED:
A Puppy's First
COME Lesson

Troubleshooting

If your dog gets distracted, try using an excited voice and turn and walk the other way. Your movement and animation make you interesting and his curiosity will bring him back to you.

If your dog doesn't come when you are outdoors, try the following suggestions:

- Fewer distractions: maybe work in the garage or on the deck.
- Better treats.
- Keep him closer when training. Most dogs have a distance beyond where you have lost influence.
- Always work in a safe area, even if he is on leash. Then when you want to try without the leash, you can drop it or let him drag it while you move away from him and let him learn to follow you or come when you call him. Letting him drag the leash gives you a better opportunity to catch him or step on it if he moves away from you instead of toward you.
- If he gets away, when he comes back do not yell or scold him. If you greet his return by scolding him, he won't be happy to be home and may reconsider coming back the next time. Keep your voice high and happy.
- Resist chasing your dog. Try luring him with a treat. Walking away will usually get his attention.
- Come is an exercise you should practice for short periods every day, in many places, with many distractions and wonderful rewards. Unlike some exercises where we may start to fade some of the food rewards, we recommend using food to reward Come every time.

Training Leave It and Want To Trade

Goal: Dog will learn self-control to resist taking a treat or object until given permission or until another treat is substituted.

Leave It and Want To Trade training exercises are very similar so they have been grouped together. Often dogs eat or pick up something they shouldn't. Leave It will prevent him from picking something up and Want To Trade will help you teach him to give it back after he has picked it up.

Show one treat to your dog.

Leave It

Level 1: Getting the Behavior

Training your dog to leave something so he can get something else is a fun and quick exercise that is easy to start.

1 Put a treat in each hand. Make a fist with your right hand with your thumb folded inside your fingers and show it to your dog while holding your left hand behind your back.

2 Most dogs will take some time to try to get to the treat in your hand, ranging from licking to literally trying to pry your fingers away with his teeth. If you are concerned your dog will bite or hurt you, wear a glove on your hand at first. Keep your right hand low enough so your dog has full access to it. Your dog does not get the original treat from your right hand, just the treat from behind your back. We want your dog to think "give up the treat to get the treat."

A dog will usually try to get to the treat you are showing him.

Training LEAVE IT
with a Trained Dog

As soon as your dog stops trying to get the first treat, give him the treat from your other hand.

3 The very second your dog stops trying to get the treat, bring your left hand out and present the treat on your palm for him to eat. Reload treats in each hand and repeat. Many dogs will stop touching your right hand in five to ten tries, understanding that if they don't touch your hand, they will get a reward.

4 Now it is time to change the order. Your left hand is now fisted in front of you with a treat and your right hand has a treat behind your back. After your dog has done this a few times, change locations, move outdoors, and change body positions from standing to sitting.

Level 2:

After a few sessions, if your dog is doing well with Level 1, try using the treat in your open palm and present it to the dog. Be prepared to close your fingers over it if he tries to get the treat. He should quickly learn this is the same exercise. The difference is he can see the treat, but he still can't have it. As soon as he turns away from the treat in front of you or resists trying to get it, give him the treat from behind your back.

Level 3: Adding a Verbal Cue and Proofing the Behavior

When you can show your dog a treat and predict he won't try to get it, it is time to add a verbal cue. The common cue is Leave It. To add the cue to the exercise, first say Leave It and then present the treat in a closed hand as you did at the beginning of the exercise. We go back to the basics because we are changing things. You should be able to progress quickly, once he understands Leave It precedes a reward for leaving the treat in front of him.

Having taught a reliable Leave It using various interesting objects like treats, toys, and even tissues, you should be able to say Leave It to your dog when something major happens and stop him in his tracks.

Want To Trade

Trade Goal: Train the dog to drop something and get a treat

Want to Trade is similar to Leave it, but it is usually used to teach a dog to drop a toy so we can throw it again. It is also used to teach the dog to drop anything you don't want her to be carrying in her mouth or chewing on.

To teach Want to Trade you will use treats and a toy or rawhide bone. You want your dog to be able to take the 'Trade' into her mouth and hold it.

There are 2 levels for training Want to Trade

Level 1: Getting the Behavior

Level 2: Adding a Verbal Cue and Proofing the Behavior

Level 1: Getting the Behavior

To teach Want to Trade you will use treats and a toy or rawhide bone. Use something your dog will take into her mouth and hold.

1 Start with a toy or rawhide bone in one hand and several small treats in the other. Show the toy to your dog and let her take one end and quickly show her the treat from the other hand. We usually start using a verbal cue right away because it works so quickly. The verbal cue we use is "Want to Trade."

Sadie is asked to trade her toy for a treat.

The dog drops the toy. You pick up the toy while the dog takes the treat from your other hand.

You give the toy back to the dog. The dog learns she gets a treat and her toy back.

2 When your dog releases the toy, deliver the treat right to her mouth. After you repeat this a few times, she might refuse to take the toy and hold out for the treats. This is when you want to escalate the attractiveness of the toy. You can switch it out for a better one or put a smudge of peanut butter or cheese on the end. Offer her the toy but hold onto the end, say the verbal cue, and offer a treat to trade.

3 After your last successful trade, let her have a double reward by giving her back the toy she traded for the treat and end your session.

On your walks after lots of practice, your dog will be able to give up something as wonderful as a dead bird, when you use your verbal cue, "Want to Trade."

By then, he knows something good will happen.

If you don't happen to be carrying treats with you, substitute a good scratch and lots of praise. When you get home, practice again a few times with really good treats. You want him to remember it is worth his while to trade, even if there isn't always an immediate treat.

Chloe is learning to walk on a loose leash.

When you teach your dog

When your dog wants to lead you off the path. Stop. Keep the leash taut and wait until your dog takes a step back. Then, loosen the leash and continue your walk.

When your dog teaches you

You are walking your dog. He sees something he wants to sniff. It is off your path, but being the kind person you are, you step towards the dog. The leash loosens. You have followed the dog to the interesting object. Good for the dog. He has just taught you!

Loose Leash Walking

Goal: walk with your dog walking calmly beside you.

If you have a dog who chronically and constantly pulls on the leash when you are walking him, it is hard for you or the dog to enjoy the exercise. Try the suggestions below and you will both look forward to your daily walks.

If you have a puppy or adult dog with no previous experience walking on a leash, you have the opportunity to teach him positive leash-walking habits.

Dogs love to explore and sniff all things. If the interesting object is out of leash range, the dog will lean into the collar to get closer. Stop and hold the leash firm, without allowing any give, so the dog is held from going where he wants to sniff. Wait until the dog backs up a step or turns to you, then allow the dog to go to his interesting object as a reward for loosening the leash.

There are some tools available that can make walking on a loose leash easier to train. One product we often use to train a loose leash walk is a Gentle Leader™ (www.gentleleader.com). It is a head halter type of collar and can be used to train a loose leash walk. Many owners continue to use this product during the lifetime of the dog. The dog quickly learns that, just like a leash, when the owner brings out the Gentle Leader™ it means a walk. There are several brands of head collar or halter available. We recommend spending some time training your dog to tolerate the head halter before using it on a walk. The fit of the product can make a big difference with its comfort and tolerance by the dog, so work with a training professional to be sure the fit is correct.

You might also consider one of several types of body harnesses, if your dog is not a candidate for a head harness collar. Working with a trainer and following the harness fitting and use instructions closely will help in the retraining.

Loose Leash Walking *Continued*

We do not recommend using collars meant to choke or threaten the dog. The choke collar, pinch or prong collars only work using pain or the the threat of pain. **Do not** use any product that causes pain or discomfort to your dog when he pulls. This can result in increased stress and he may become more fearful or anxious about his surroundings, including other dogs, children and strangers.

"Be a Tree" is one technique used to teach a dog to walk nicely on a leash. This entails standing still immediately when your dog starts to pull on the leash. When the dog relieves the tightness on the leash, you move forward with your dog. This works best if the leash is short and the dog only has the opportunity to move a foot or so in any direction. If you use a longer leash, the communication with the dog is slower.

Training with the Gentle Leader Head Halter

Jake is being introduced to the Gentle Leader™ head halter.

Paula Says

There are many techniques, books and DVDs available that trainers and owners use to teach loose leash walking.

"My Dog Pulls. What Do I Do?" by Turid Rugaas (www.turidrugaas.com) is a book I would recommend. Clicker training can also help with pulling dogs.

Visit www.clickertraining.com for great information to help you.

Training LOOSE LEASH WALKING: A Young Dog's First Lesson

Body harnesses are an option if your dog has problems with a head halter collar.

131

> **Puppies under the age of six months should not stay in crates longer than four hours.**
>
> If the puppy is home alone, arrange to come home for lunch or find a neighbor or friend who can let him out to potty during the day.
>
> If you have been consistent and have not approached your dog when he whines during the training process, chances are if he whines at night, he really does have to potty. Take him directly outside, let him do his job, and go directly back to the crate. No play or cuddle time, or he will start getting you up every night.
>
> Never punish, scold, or bang on the crate to get your dog to stop making noise. It will stress him, frighten him, or reward him with attention for his efforts.
>
> Dogs like schedules. Once you establish a night time schedule and a daytime pattern, your dog will start to predict bedtime and crate time and may even enter the crate before you give a cue.

Crate Training Your New Dog/Puppy

Crate training is recommended to help you housetrain your pet and manage your new pet's access throughout your home while he's learning manners and self-control.

A crate is a useful tool that your pet can be happy in when properly introduced to it. Some of the frequent uses are: safe traveling, a 'time-out' place for calming disruptive or inappropriate behavior, a 'den' when you have a houseful of people who aren't all comfortable with dogs or a way to keep your pet comfortable when he's in a home where pets aren't welcome. Whatever the reason, if you properly train your pet to use his crate, he'll be happy in it and you'll be glad to have it as an option when needed.

(For Housetraining a Puppy Using a Crate see Chapter 7.)

Timing: Your dog may learn quickly or take longer. The dog's age, disposition and experience are important. A puppy who has had no previous experience with a crate may take to it easier than an older dog for whom a crate may have an unpleasant association, for example a dog rescued from a puppy mill. When training, be sure you are making each step pleasant, with treats and praise. A crate is misused if an owner depends on it exclusively for confinement and housetraining.

Selecting a Crate

Crates may be plastic or metal pens that are collapsible. They come in various sizes and can be purchased from most pet supply stores. The small light plastic ones may not be sturdy enough to hold a growing large-breed puppy. Invest in a sturdy, appropriate crate that will work for your dog's adult size.

Introducing Your Dog to the Crate

Place the crate in an area of your house where the family spends a lot of time. Put a soft blanket or towel in the crate. Talk to your dog in a happy voice as you bring him over to the crate. If you are using a metal crate with a sliding pan as the floor, we recommend putting a thin rug or towel under the pan to reduce any rattling noise that could startle your dog when he first steps in. Also, place a soft blanket or towel over the pan to add comfort. Make sure the crate door is open and secured so it won't hit your dog and frighten him.

At night, we recommend putting the crate in the bedroom of an adult, at least while the dog is getting used to it. Crating a dog away from the family will often cause him stress or anxiety and he may whine, bark, howl, yodel or bay. Once your dog gets used to being crated at night, you can begin moving the crate a little at a time to your preferred location. It is important to keep puppies within hearing distance at night since they may need to go outside to potty.

Place a soft blanket or towel in the bottom of your dog's crate to make it more comfortable.

Crating your puppy near you at night helps housetraining by letting you hear his signals when he needs to go out.

CRATE Training:
A Young Dog's
First Lesson

133

Crate Training Your New Dog/Puppy *Continued*

Toss treats and toys in the crate to encourage the puppy to enter. Never force him.

Be sure the gate is out of the way in case he backs up.

Soon the puppy will be comfortably entering the crate to get the treat. Practice. Crate train slowly following the guideline given here.

The crate should always be associated with something pleasant. Put treats and toys in the crate so the dog has to walk in to get them. Let him become comfortable entering and leaving the crate. Do not force him to enter the crate. Give him time to figure it out. It may take some time but it will be so helpful later in the training. When the dog does stay in the crate continue to give him treats dropping them in the back of the crate. If he comes out, the treats go away. Start again in a few minutes.

You can also shut the dog outside the crate to build his interest in the treats inside and make him want to enter the crate.

Try feeding meals in the crate and leaving the door open. When it's clear that the dog is comfortable in the crate, close the door while he's eating. Open it when he's finished, as long as he is not barking or whining. Gradually extend the time the door is closed. With each meal your dog eats with the door closed, add a few minutes to the time he stays in the closed crate after the meal. If he gets stressed, barks, whines or digs at the crate, shorten the time he's in the crate with the door closed. Never open the door while he is making noise.

Do not approach or release your dog while he is whining, barking or digging at the door of the crate. You want him to learn that quiet, calm behavior brings humans to him, and barking or whining makes humans freeze or back up.

Crate train slowly, watching for fear, stress or anxiety in your dog. If you see him showing concern, back the training up to a place he is comfortable and stop. Continue later in the day, starting with the basics and quickly moving back to the spot your dog showed stress.

Next, begin training your dog to go into the crate BEFORE you give the treat or set the food bowl down. Practice with him for about five pieces of food. Then wait. Even if he takes just ONE step toward the crate, reward him by tossing the treat in the crate. He will start to figure out if he goes in by himself, you will reward and praise him. Give him a BIG reward, multiple pieces of food or treats, for going in on his own, always putting the treats in the crate. Call him back out, but do not give him a treat. When you can look at the crate and he walks in, start putting a verbal cue with this behavior. Use words like "kennel", "in," "go to bed," or anything that makes sense to you.

Take the training a step further by giving your dog a treat, shutting the crate door and walking out of sight. Come back to the crate before he starts to stress. Release him from the crate but do not give him a treat. Practice sending him to his crate and moving out of sight, but stay in the house. When he can stay in the crate calmly for ten minutes or so, go out the door you normally exit, count to five, and return. Be very calm and matter of fact when leaving and coming back in. We want this to become routine, even boring for the dog. Repeat this process several times a day. With each repetition, vary the length of time you leave him. Don't be predictable. This may take several days or several weeks.

Home Alone

When your dog can spend thirty minutes or so in the crate without becoming anxious or afraid, you can begin leaving him crated for short periods when you are away from the house.

Crate him using your cue and a treat as a reward after he enters. You might also want to leave a toy in the crate. Be sure the toy is something he can't chew into pieces while you are gone. Most dogs do fine with Kong® toys

filled with treats or kibble. Have several Kongs® prepared and in the freezer. Give these to your dog when you leave. He will stay busy getting the treats out as they thaw.

Leave and come home calmly. Only approach the crate if your dog is calm. If he has made a mess, don't scold or punish him, just take him outdoors as you normally do when you come home.

Crate your dog for short periods when you are home. You do not need to do this every day, just from time to time. You don't want your dog to associate crating with being left alone. The crate should be a bedroom, not a jail.

> **Never put your dog in the crate for punishment or when you are angry with him.**

Some puppies learn quickly to take a treat and enter a crate for another treat.

Dog Tales

Wrong Way

Here is how to crate train all wrong. Many years ago the first puppy I raised using a crate was a tiny Field Spaniel puppy. Her mother was ill, so she came to live with us younger than normal. She was thin and wormy, and it took a while to get her healthy.

A friend had recommended crate training for housetraining and it seemed like a great idea. She even loaned us a metal crate, so we set the crate up in the living room and gave her some bedding, toys, and water, expecting her to be happy and sleep through the night. Wrong. She cried, whined, and was miserable for three nights, so my husband and I were miserable, too. The fourth night she quieted down and slept, so that was a relief.

The crate was for an adult dog, so she happily used one end to potty and the other to sleep and play. I was learning the hard way that crate training took some knowledge, timing and common sense. The puppy turned out great, and I am still using the lessons learned long ago to help other people crate train their pups.

Rewarding or Reinforcing Behavior

By understanding reinforcement, you will see you are not forever bound to carry a pocketful of treats. Your pet will soon be working for your verbal praise. He wants to please you and he knows he will occasionally get a treat, too.

Take advantage of the many small opportunities to reinforce your dog's behavior. You may have him Sit before letting him out the door, before petting him, or before giving him his food. Remember to always praise him and offer a treat when appropriate.

When your pet is learning a new behavior, he should be rewarded every time he does the behavior. This is called continuous reinforcement. It may be necessary to use "shaping," with your pet. Shaping is defined as reinforcing something close to the desired response and gradually requiring more before he gets the treat. For example, if you are training your dog to shake hands, you may initially reward him for lifting his paw off the ground, then for lifting it higher, then for touching your hand, then for letting you hold his paw and finally, for actually shaking hands with you.

Intermittent reinforcement can start to be used once your pet has reliably learned a behavior. At first, you may reward him with the treat three times out of four, then about half the time, then a third of the time and so forth, until you are only rewarding him occasionally with the treat. Continue to praise him every time, although once he's learned the behavior, the praise can be a quiet positive, "Good boy." Pairing the treats with praise early in the training makes the praise alone more effective.

Crate Issues

Q **Caller:** *Indy is our Beagle, age three, and we adopted him from the Animal Rescue League. He had been relinquished by his two previous owners. He cowers when we scold our other pets, so we suspect he had been abused previously. He's a great dog and seldom does anything wrong.*

However, if he knows we are about to put him in his crate before we leave the house, he hides. When I try to pick him up, he bares his teeth. The other day, my boyfriend picked up our other to dog to carry him to his crate. Indy was on the floor at my feet, partially under a blanket. When I tried to pick him up, he bared his teeth and growled. Later, when my boyfriend tried to pick him up, he snapped and barked at him. I ended up putting on his collar and leash and dragged him to the crate.

Normally, he is the sweetest dog. It breaks my heart to think what was done to him that he gets so frightened. Any suggestions?

A **Paula says:** *His crate obviously isn't his favorite place, so let's start there. Feed his meals in the crate, and offer extra treats and his toys there. Just put them in the crate and let him go in and get them. He should be in the crate sometimes when you are home, even for a short time, so he doesn't equate the crate with your absence. If the only time he is in the crate is when you are gone, he associates the hurried activity of being dragged into the crate as stressful. Ideally, we want him running to the crate on a verbal cue, so he voluntarily enters it, gets a treat and a stuffed Kong® to work on while you are gone.*

While you are working on the crate enrichment program, put him in the crate calmly with lots of reward for twenty to thirty minutes before you leave. Try to keep his fear/anxiety level below where he feels he has to threaten you. Use a calm voice, even tones, and lots of treats.

Try not to pick him up or reach for his collar. Rather, keep a leash on him that he can drag around or use a loop made out of your leash to help guide him to the crate.

Notes: *This is a common problem with dogs and new owners. Owners may assume the dog "knows" to go to the crate, and they don't realize how stressed the dog has become. Grabbing for the collar makes the dog defensive. In "dog-speak," a snap, snarl, or bite are your dog's way to communicate. Training a puppy to tolerate or even like the collar being handled is a wonderful exercise that should be included in any puppy class.*
Refer to Crate Training on page 132.

For more information on clicker training, go to www.clickertraining.com.

It is easy to learn and the whole family can participate by using this technique.

The clicker shown is one of the most popular. It is available at the ARL or local pet stores.

—Dog Facts—

Dogs can sense frequencies of 30,000 times per second. Humans can detect sounds at 20,000 times per second.

A dog's smell is 100,000 times stronger than a human's depending on the dog breed.

Clicker Training

The basic premise of clicker training is to teach the dog that the click means a reward is due.

When the behavior is clicked and the dog is rewarded, he will try to repeat that behavior for more rewards. The click is the communication link that lets the dog know exactly what he did that was rewarded. Often by the time you say "good dog," your dog has already changed behaviors and may believe he is being rewarded for that behavior.

Always separate the click and the treat by about 1/2 second. If you click and treat at the same the dog can become confused. Click first, and then treat to make it clear to the dog.

Note: If you click, no matter whether you intended to, or you mistakenly clicked the wrong thing, reward the dog anyway. Once you start clicker training, we want the dog to be very confident that click equals reward, every time.

The click can be used to help a dog start a new behavior. An example might be training a dog to spin to the right. You can use a treat to help the dog turn his head to the right and when he does, click/treat. Repeat about three to five times, click/treat each time. Then wait and see if the dog will offer a head turn on his own. Be ready to click/treat him when he does. Soon the dog will be offering the head turn readily, be sure to continue the click/treat.

Some people are concerned that they will need to carry a clicker forever. Clickers are used to start training a new behavior and once the behavior is on cue, the clicker can be phased out.

The clicker is only the bridge to the reward. It is the signal that you are telling your dog, "that was right; good dog; here's a reward."

Positive Reinforcement

Also key to clicker training is to understand positive reinforcement. Be sure the reward you are using is actually rewarding to the dog. If your dog does not enjoy a pat on the head, he will not view it as a reward for his behavior. When you teach any new behavior, you will depend heavily on food as the primary reinforcer and the clicker or the phrase "good dog" or "yes" as the secondary or conditioned reinforcer. As the dog learns the behavior and its associated cues, whether verbal or physical, you will start to use the clicker less and praise more. Often we start to randomly and variably reinforce the behavior.

If you choose clicker training, it may start with luring a Sit with a treat. The dog's rear is heading toward the floor, click, and then quickly offer the food reward as the dog sits on the floor.

After you have lured the Sit approximately five times and followed with click/treat, try standing still and see if the dog offers you the Sit behavior. If he does, click and give a reward. If he doesn't, lure the Sit a few more times and try again. Once the dog offers the behavior several times in a row, stop using a treat in the "lure" hand and keep the treats in your clicker hand. Your "lure" hand now becomes a cue behavior for the dog. Using the same gesture you did when you had the treat in the hand, see if the dog offers Sit. When he does, click and reward him. You have just taught a hand signal to your dog for Sit.

Whatever method you use, training should be enjoyable and fun for both the dog and the pet owner. We recommend encouraging your children to participate in the training, especially tricks so they can show the dog off and enjoy practicing.

Positive reinforcement in the form of treats and praise is key to all training, including clicker training.

139

Topics:

General Health and Well-Being

Usually we think we can tell if there is something wrong with our dogs.

The concern is many dogs cannot or will not spell out their discomfort. Check your dog over daily, looking for warm or cold spots, lumps, limping, hair loss, unusual or unpleasant odors, or anything that is different from what you have noticed before.

Check your dog over daily

Eyes and nose. Check his eyes and nose. If there is a discharge that isn't the normal clear tear-like discharge, start looking for other problems. Discharges that are thick and have a color can indicate an infection. Dogs have their noses everywhere and can be exposed to injury, infections, or even weeds and seeds that can become lodged in the soft tissues. Itchy noses can be the start of upper respiratory infections, injury, or something else out of place.

Hair loss and itchy skin. Hair loss and itchy skin are reasons to visit your vet. Hair loss, especially around the eyes and lips can be the start of a skin infection. Many things can cause both symptoms, including allergies, ringworm and mange fleas, to name a few. While not an emergency, you will want to get these symptoms checked by your vet for the comfort and health of your dog. If your dog sleeps with you and is itchy, you won't get much sleep, because he will be licking, scratching and chewing off and on all night.

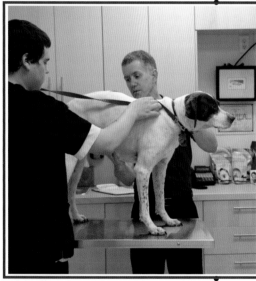

Take a list of questions with you when taking your dog to the veterinarian.

Lumps. Lumps should always be checked by your veterinarian. With lumps, especially under the jaw, in the "arm pits" or belly, don't wait thinking they will go away or get smaller. Have them checked while they are small in case they turn out to be something serious.

Odor. A distinctively smelly discharge or odor from your dog's rear should also be checked. It could be anal gland infections or other problems. This can be painful for the dog. Butt-scooting or excessive licking of the tail, flank, or genital area can signal anal gland problems. Butt-scooting can also be caused by worms or fleas, so it is definitely something to get checked.

Limping. Limping is a concern but might not be an emergency unless you know for a fact your dog was injured. Always contact your veterinarian. He may recommend X-rays to diagnose the symptoms. In some young dogs, the limping may seem to change legs, side to side, or even front to back. This can be a painful condition called panosteitis, indicating "growing pains" or "wandering lameness."

Gums and teeth. During your exam, check your dog's gums and teeth, something he should be readily willing to let you do. Gums should be pink, but not pale pink and not bright pink. Check regularly so you will know what his normal color should be. Some dogs have black gums and even black or dark tongues, so noticing a change may be more difficult. The color can change with exercise, exposure to heat, injury, or disease. If you see a change in gum color, contact your veterinarian. The dog's teeth will yellow with age, but if you see tarter, dark layers of stuff building up on the gum line, talk to your vet about options. A dental scaling by your veterinarian usually requires full anesthesia and is worth trying to delay or prevent. Some dogs that regularly chew bones or other chewing toys may have less tartar.

Ask your veterinarian about other prevention ideas. Using a toothbrush and special canine dental paste can be a good way to go. Your dog may not enjoy it at first, so start slowly with the brush, doing a few teeth at a time. Many dogs like the taste of the doggy toothpaste, and don't resist it. You can also use a washcloth with the toothpaste. Try to work your way back to the large molars in the rear of his mouth. He may work against you by doing a chewing motion with his jaws, so be careful where you put your fingers in his mouth.

Your veterinary visits will routinely include your vet checking your dog's:

ears

glands

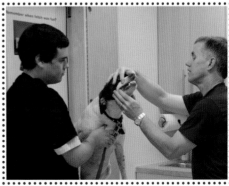

gums and teeth

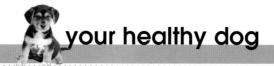

General Health and Well-Being *Continued*

Toenails. Your dog's toenails should be checked and clipped every two weeks. If you are comfortable clipping your dog's toenails, we find it is best to do after a bath, or even in the bathtub as the toenails are soft and less likely to have a sharp edge. If the dog is still in the bathtub, they may stand more quietly than if they are laying on the floor with you. Make sure you are using nail clippers designed specifically for pets. Clip off the tip of the nail, being careful not to clip the vein running through it.

Ears. Take a peek into your dog's ears each week. Sniff to see if there is a yeasty or unpleasant odor. If you notice this, be sure your veterinarian checks it to see what treatment will work best. Don't try to treat an ear infection without getting it diagnosed as some of the over the counter remedies can make an infection worse or cause your dog pain instead of helping the problem. Use a cotton ball with ear cleaning solution or a baby wipe to clean the inside of your dog's ears. Do not force your finger or a Q-tip into the ear canal.

Heartworm. Schedule an annual examination with your veterinarian. Your dog should be tested for heartworm, which is carried by infected mosquitoes, and receive a monthly preventative. The cost of the testing and preventative may seem pricey, especially if you have a large dog or several dogs, but treatment for heartworm is much costlier and can be very hard on your dog. It is just not worth the risk.

Preventive monthly treatment for your dog is effective and, depending on the brand, can also help keep your dog from being infected with other internal parasites like hookworms and roundworms, which can both be infectious to humans as well as dogs. Work with your veterinarian for the best option for your pet.

Sometimes your pet just doesn't seem right. Maybe he didn't eat supper or didn't eat as much as usual. Maybe

According to www.heartwormsociety.org, most areas of the United States have cases of heartworm.

The farther south you go, the greater the concentration of the infections. When we brought so many dogs into rescue groups from Hurricane Katrina, it seemed nearly all the dogs had heartworm infections.

A routine visit to the veterinarian will include a check-up of your dog's heart and skin. You may also be asked to bring in a stool sample.

he is walking a bit slower on his walk, or doesn't want to play ball or seems grumpy. How do you know when there is something serious? Call your veterinarian's office and ask the person who answers the phone. She has been specially trained to get the information from you and help you and your veterinarian decide what might be an emergency. Many things can wait until morning, but bleeding, injuries to eyes or internal organs and broken bones cannot.

Take a list of questions with you when you take your dog to the veterinarian, or you may forget to ask them when you are there.

General Grooming

Bathing. Most dogs only need to be bathed every two to three months, unless they have rolled in something smelly. Ask your vet or groomer if you want to bathe your dog more often.

Brushing. Brush your dog three to four times a week, no matter the length of his coat. This will get rid of dead skin and distribute the natural oils for a shiny coat. It also helps with shedding.

First Aid Situations

Would you know what to do if your pet was bleeding or choking? Some things that happen can be emergencies and you can help your pet before getting him to the veterinarian. We recommend checking into First Aid classes offered specifically for pets by the American Red Cross. Refer to Getting Ready for Your New Dog, First Aid Kit on page 56 for a list of first aid supplies to have on hand.

Troubleshooting

I get questions from owners whose dogs have become aggressive and threatening to bite "suddenly" or "out of the blue."

- My first suggestion is a veterinary check, because many times a sudden behavior change can have a basis in a medical issue.

- Old age or injury can cause a normally tolerant dog to suddenly be defensive or grouchy.

- There are some great medications that can help with pain and can keep dogs comfortable while they heal or if they are dealing with arthritis.

Always keep a pet first aid kit stocked and ready for emergencies.

Choosing A Veterinarian

We get many calls from dog owners who do not have a regular veterinarian. They might call about a behavior that concerns them and we often counsel them to get the dog checked for medical issues that can manifest as behavior problems.

Here is what to look for in a veterinarian, staff, and clinic:

Friendly. The staff should greet you by name when you walk in the door, or they should at least know your dog's name.

Lets you stay with your dog. You may want to be able to stay with your dog during the exam and vaccinations, but some clinics routinely remove the dog from your presence to the back of the clinic for vaccinations, exam, and toenail trims. If this is not your preference, talk to the veterinarian and ask to stay with your dog.

Tells you your options. Before treatment, know your options. Will the treatment be different if they do more tests? Does the cost of more testing become a factor if the condition is serious?

Health Check Up

Q **Caller:** *We recently adopted a Cocker Spaniel named Molly.*

The other family gave her up because she bit their child who was trying to take away a bone. We were told this was an isolated event and that she is a sweet dog. We don't have small children, but have been looking for a little buddy for our dog. We have been trying to be patient and loving but it has been a nightmare.

If she doesn't want to go out and we try to get her out, she literally attacks us. She hates my son and barks and snaps at him. Whenever we leave, she pees or poops on the floor, despite having just been out. We can't even play with our other dog without her barking and snapping at him. I am reluctant to give her to anyone, yet I don't know how long we want to keep her. Can you help?

A **Paula says:** *While it is possible the family you got her from just didn't give you the real details with her, I have to wonder what else might be going on with her. You didn't mention her health records and hopefully they kept her vaccinated and groomed so she is healthy. Spaniels are so susceptible to ear infections, and under stress they can become much worse very quickly. If you haven't taken her to your veterinarian, that is the first place to go. If she checks out medically, then we can start talking about her fear issues and trying to help her become more comfortable with your son and husband.*

Follow-up: *We decided to give Molly some time and in the interim, I took her to the vet. It turns out she had a bad ear infection. We treated her and she has been a wonderful dog ever since.*

Choosing A Veterinarian *Continued*

Focuses on the dog and you. The staff and veterinarian should be friendly and personable, and treat you and your dog as their only concern during your time together.

Gets down to the dog's level. Other pluses are staff and even veterinarians who will get down to the dog's level if the dog is not comfortable on the exam table.

Cleanliness. If you walk in and something smells bad or looks dirty, be concerned. Much of veterinary medicine is done in sterile conditions and if the lobby and exam rooms are not kept clean (not necessarily sterile), chances are the rest of the clinic is not clean. If there has just been a potty accident or something was spilled in the back, staff should be quick to explain.

A veterinarian's office should be clean. The staff should be friendly and knowledgeable.

Dog Tales

We took our Lab, Shady, who was having trouble walking, to the the vet. The vet sat on the floor with her head in his hands, gently examining her. This was a clinic that is routinely open late in the day, and the vet's two-year-old son came in to visit us, too. He sat cross-legged on the floor, just like Dad, and bowed his head over Shady until his forehead rested on her shoulder. I looked at Dad, wondering what he was doing. The vet said he wasn't sure why he does that but each time he did, the dog got better. Works for me!

As we exited the clinic, Shady was gaining strength and steadier on her feet. I was thrilled she was doing better. We had some pain pills and she did get much better in a few days, and while the toddler probably didn't "fix" her, he didn't hurt anything. It was a sweet casual clinic experience that meant a lot to me.

Vaccinations

Your veterinarian is your best guide to what vaccinations to give your dog and when they are needed. For legal purposes, do not let your dog's rabies vaccination become overdue. Rabies is a disease that is lethal to humans and can be transmitted by any warm-blooded mammal.

Many people assume indoor dogs cannot catch rabies, but one of the biggest problem carriers of rabies can be bats. Bats can get into nearly any home and expose you and your pets to rabies. If you find a bat in your home, testing it through a public health office is highly recommended, not only for your pet's sake, but also for yours. Any public office that requires your pet to be licensed will require a rabies vaccination to be current in order to license your pet. Check with your veterinarian or local authorities for your location's ordinances.

Other vaccinations do not expire on a particular day or date, but the reminders from your vet provide good guidelines. Again, check with your veterinarian on which vaccinations are appropriate for your pet. If you do not travel to a tick-populated area, you won't need the vaccinations associated with them. If you board your dog or take him anywhere multiple dogs might congregate, you will want to consider Bordatella vaccinations, which help protect from the canine disease commonly called kennel cough. You will want your dog vaccinated for commonly communicated diseases like canine distemper, infectious canine hepatitis and parvovirus. Follow your veterinarian's recommendations.

What Diseases Can Humans Get from Dogs?

Good hygiene and maintaining healthy pets will prevent us from catching diseases or parasites from them. Some people may be more at risk if they have lowered immune systems. All dogs should be routinely examined for internal and external parasites. Dog can harbor roundworms, a parasite that can infect people and cause skin problems, blindness or organ damage. A family with members who may be at risk should consult with the family doctor before adding a pet. For more information about Zoonotic Diseases (diseases that can be passed to humans from animals), check the American Veterinary Medical Association website at www.avma.org.

Hot cars are deadly

Do not leave a dog in a hot car—even for a "minute." Hot cars become deadly for dogs in less than 30 minutes when the outside temperature is 85-degrees. Even on a 75-degree day, the temperature in a car can soar, even when in the shade with a window open.

If you see a dog left in a car on a hot day, try to locate the owner. Take down the car make, color and license plate. Ask store owners to help, or call animal control or the police for assistance.

If your dog shows symptoms of heatstroke - heavy panting, loss of appetite, lethargy, a rapid heartbeat, lack of coordination or vomiting - call your vet immediately.

Some happy endings

from the Animal Rescue League of Iowa

Sadie

Working on this book, we spent many days at ARL. One day, Robin, an ARL volunteer came by to say hello. We broke into a smile at the tail-wagging Dachshund trotting along with her. Robin introduced us to Sadie who was on her way to WHO-TV as pet of the week. Sadie, age 14, had been dropped-off in ARL's overnight pet box with no information.

The veterinarian examined her. Rotted front teeth had to be removed. She was covered with bites. But, other than neglect, Sadie was healthy. I couldn't get her out of my mind.

My husband and I have an 8-year-old Labrador we rescued. Although he prefers large dogs, as a boy, he loved a Dachshund. I started 'talking' to him about Sadie. He agreed to go to ARL and to bring our Lab, Kayla for a compatibility visit.

I called ARL to ask if anyone had adopted Sadie after her TV appearance. The answer was, "No." My fear was that as a 14 year-old dog, Sadie would have a harder time finding a home. I knew I wasn't going to leave ARL without her.

Sadie's now been with us over a year and often is with me at work. She's a very special lady, loves everyone and is happiest on a lap. Her sight is failing and she sleeps a lot. But, when you see her running as fast as she can across a country field or vying with the Lab for a toy that's bigger than she is, she has everyone smiling.

Jeramy

Lilly

Before we met Lilly, she worked for a living. For 4-1/2 years, Lilly earned her keep in a cage in a puppy mill, giving birth to litter after litter of puppies that were taken away as soon as possible and sold. Perhaps that's why when Lilly came to our home, she was so attached to her stuffed animal "babies."

We adopted Lilly from ARL more than 11 years ago. She walked out of our lives not long ago – haltingly, in failing health, but with the patience and good spirits that endeared her to all who met her.

Family photographs were never complete unless she was in them. She never met anyone who wasn't a friend. She wanted to be part of every gathering, even though she never had much to say. But, that was another of her strengths. She was a great listener.

A two-legged friend once said, "Lilly won the dog lottery—comfortable blankets and beds to lie on, plenty of toys to chew on, plenty of treats to nibble on and someone always ready to scratch her stomach." Yet, we, her human family were enriched in ways people who have never had a dog can't understand. We will always remember our furry friend.

The house isn't the same.

The Evans Family

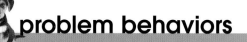

Topics:

Barking

Question: "Help! My dog barks all the time, and we are so tired of it. How do we stop him from barking?"

Answer: Of course, some barking is normal. Dogs bark. Barking when a car pulls into the driveway or when an especially loud truck or motorcycle goes by is normal. Most dogs are territorial and will sound an alarm if unique sounds or people come to the door. Some dogs are very stimulated by movement or motion and will bark when they see something moving. Dogs may get bored hanging out in the backyard alone or inside all day while you are gone. Barking can be a self-rewarding behavior, just as some people talk more than others.

What becomes abnormal, obnoxious or dangerous is when the owner has no control to stop the dog, or the dog barks for long periods of time, or adds other aggressive behaviors like lunging and snapping with the barking.

Often owners think the problem will go away on its own. The dog will grow out of it, learn a better behavior, and the owners won't have to work on the problem. That plan will not work.

What we want to do is examine the behavior, try to decide what reinforcement the dog is getting from doing that behavior, and then try to change the situation so the behavior is either modified or eliminated. A few questions can help us decide where we should focus our efforts. Often the behavior, now considered a huge problem, has grown over time from a fairly small problem.

> **Paula Says**
>
> If your dog's barking is a serious problem, work with a trainer or behavior counselor.

What is your Dog Barking At?

Of course, he isn't really barking at everything, it just seems like it. Looking out the window, watching people walking by, children on bikes, dogs being walked, cars, motorcycles, or joggers can set your dog to barking. For most dogs, any movement is stimulating and can cause the dog to become interested in either chasing what is moving or insisting it keeps moving off the dog's territory.

In the fenced-in backyard, running the fences and barking at the dogs on the other side can be problematic for several reasons. While it may seem like good exercise for the dog, it raises his adrenaline level and probably his stress level. Some dogs can stay playful and friendly during fence running, but many dogs become increasingly frustrated, both with the fence and with the other dog.

Squirrels, other rodents and even birds in the backyard can also stimulate barking. Almost always, barking is stimulated by motion.

Almost all barking is stimulated by movement.

Troubleshooting

We have worked with owners who have had problems with their local animal control agency because of a neighbor's complaints about the dog's barking.

- Most animal control agencies have specific regulations about barking, including how long it lasts.

- If you have a neighbor issue, talk to other neighbors, and see if they are frustrated. If not, see if they will write a short note that your dog is not a problem for them. Explain you are working on it and hope to improve things shortly. Thank them for their patience.

- **If appropriate** ask your vet for a short note stating that your dog is current on vaccinations, friendly, and not a danger to anyone. A professional statement will help if you go to court.

- Work with a trainer or behavior counselor. Even if you are just starting, ask for a note that states they have been hired to help solve a barking problem.

- Keep a journal of how long your dog barks when outside and at what. Videotape him. It is a great tool to have in court.

Alarm barking may begin with the doorbell ringing or the letter carrier dropping off the mail.

Reasons for Barking

Territorial or alarm barking - Stimulated by doorbells, passersby, knocking on the door, loud noises outside.

What may begin as territorial or alarm barking tends to grow into bigger and more obnoxious behavior. The dog feels his actions are being reinforced because the thing he is barking at leaves, for example the letter carrier. When you try to correct the dog by scolding or yelling at him, he might actually think you are helping, joining in, or backing him up with the noise you are making.

Without guidance and input in the form of training, behavior modification, and even environmental modifications from the owner, these behaviors escalate. The dog becomes more stimulated and from the number of reported bites to letter carriers every year, the dog will often resort to biting. See Behavior Modification below for some simple changes that can help keep everyone safe.

Motion Barking - Stimulated by people, dogs, cars, squirrels, kids, skateboarders, bikers and joggers, etc.

Some owners become nervous when walking their dog on a leash in public because their dog barks at people, animals and cars. They worry the neighbors will think they have a dangerous dog or that he is a nuisance. Often owners will either stop walking the dog altogether, relying on the back yard for the dog's exercise, or they start walking early or late, trying to avoid anything that stimulates their dog to bark. Again, motion starts the barking.

Boredom - Stimulated by needing something to do.

Solutions to Barking

Behavior Modification with Training

Changing your dog's behavior starts with you. Are you accidentally rewarding the dog's behavior by your response? Phrases like "It's OK" or yelling at your dog can actually encourage barking. Even giving the dog a bone to chew on instead of barking at a jogger may teach him to be vigilant about joggers, not because they are dangerous but because they bring rewards.

Redirect

Get your dog to return to you, or at least turn his head away from the window or stimulating object and THEN, when he's not barking reward the dog. He is rewarded for the last thing he did, which in this case was coming to or looking at you. That should at least momentarily stop the barking and give you the opportunity to redirect the dog's behavior to a toy or other activity.

If he leaves it to go back to barking, keep repeating your exercise, call him, or make an interesting noise. Reward his attention and redirect him to a behavior you can reward. Some dogs respond well if you walk to where they are barking out the window or door, calmly say, "Yes, I see that" and walk away, patting your leg and asking your dog to come with you.

Decide on an alternative behavior you would like to have your dog perform. If he loves toys, teach him to go get a toy on a cue like, "Where's your toy?" Teach the cue separately before you try using it to redirect him from a doorbell. Practice in sets of ten, maybe giving a treat as well as playing with the toy for a few seconds if he brings it to you or goes to find it. When he is successfully getting the toy on a cue at least eight out of ten times, gently and quietly have someone knock on your front door. He may start to go to the door or bark. In a happy excited voice, say your cue phrase of, "Where's your toy?" Make it easy for him at first, practicing in sets of ten so you can easily keep

track that he is being successful. Very gradually increase the sound of the knock on the door. If at any point he gets too excited and barks more than two or three times, soften the sound of the knock, going back to a point where he was successful.

Plan on this training taking several weeks, working a few times a day or as you have the chance. If someone rings your doorbell before the training is completed, you may lose some steps, so you might direct people to a different door to enter, or even disengage your doorbell until you are ready to train with it.

> ## Troubleshooting
>
> Acknowledging your dog's concern, but quickly redirecting him to another behavior can help diffuse his reaction to things outdoors that stimulate him.

Add "Quiet" Cue

If you have taught your dog to "speak" on a cue, you can add "quiet" to this trick. Practice "speak" but don't reward it. When your dog stops barking, even if it is to take a breath, deliver a treat right to his mouth and use a cue like "quiet" at the same time. Keep delivering treats about one per second as long as he is quiet. After about 5 treats, stop giving them, take a step back and say "speak" again. If he barks, that is good, then say "quiet" and if the dog has stopped barking, again deliver a treat directly to his mouth. Hopefully, he doesn't bark with his mouth full. You have started teaching a new behavior that has a cue you can use when you need it.

Gentle Leader Headcollar™

Another modification and training tool that can be useful is a Gentle Leader Headcollar™. You can use the GL headcollar in the house with a leash attached. Practice using the leash and the GL to close your dog's mouth so he can't physically bark by **gently** pulling straight UP on the leash. His nose will go up, closing his mouth and you have stopped the bark. As soon as the bark stops, release the GL pressure, and give a treat for "quiet." The point with this technique is to stop the behavior and reward an alternative behavior.

Fit for this product is vital. It is sold with a DVD describing fit and usage, so be sure to watch it if you aren't working with a trainer to get your dog started. The Gentle Leader can also be a great tool on walks if your dog is stimulated by moving objects, children or animals.

Environment and Social Stimulation

If it appears your dog barks for his own entertainment, he is either bored or likes the sound of his own voice.

You need to provide your dog with environmental and social stimulation.

- Attend a training class or find a class that teaches tricks, agility, or some other fun activity. If your dog already knows some tricks practice a bit every day. Get the kids involved. They get very creative and will love showing off the dog to their friends. Props like a play tunnel, hoop, even a broomstick work for teaching the dog to go through, under or around. Tricks like sit pretty, high 5, roll over, spin right or left, are quick to teach and fun for the dog.

- Scatter his food in the grass or even in the snow, if he can be outside for a while. Let him use his nose to hunt his own food. Dogs love to sniff and anything you can do to give him the opportunity to use his nose is great. Use Kong® toys or other toys that hold treats or food, and put several around the house for him to find. It is a great way for him to get his meals. Kong® makes a toy that "wobbles" with a hole on the side that he will have to tip over and over to get the food out.

- Manners Minder™ is a remote treat delivery system that holds a cup or so of food or treats. It can be triggered by you with a remote or by a timer on the machine.

- Play dates with other dogs are great. Compatible play styles are important or the play can become too stressful for your dog. So if your Lab likes to grab collars, and body-slam the other dog, don't pick a miniature poodle as a playmate. Often friends or neighbors have a dog like yours that will enjoy and benefit from a couple of play dates a week. An hour of play time can really tire out a dog. It is good for your dog mentally as well as physically, because of the social aspect of playing with another dog.

- Walks are good, but vary your route. The backyard time doesn't really help as far as entertainment, exercise, or stimulation since most dogs know every blade of grass, bug and rodent nest in their own yard.

Change in Environment to Reduce Barking

Along with modifying his behavior, sometimes a change in his environment can really help, such as blocking access to a door or window. Drawn drapes or moving a sofa can change the environment enough to help calm your dog's behavior. Background noise can help diffuse the noise outside.

What if your dog starts to bark right away when you leave the house?

Ignore this, if possible. You might want to set up a video recorder to see if the dog barks for long. Often dogs bark until they can no longer hear the car. Then they settle down to wait. If you videotape him and he barks longer, you will want to contact a dog expert to help. This may be a symptom of separation anxiety, or it may just be the dog is bored and needs more exercise and entertainment when you are gone. If you normally have a TV, stereo, or radio on when you are home, you might want to leave it on when you leave. The familiar background sounds can be comforting.

No matter why your dog is barking, you will want to practice coming and going, using the same pattern each time, picking up keys, purse, or briefcase. Ignore the dog or give him a treat and put him in his crate or confinement area a few minutes before you leave. While it is tempting to wait until the last second to confine your dog, that can raise his anxiety or make him try to avoid you at that time. If your dog becomes defensive, growls or protests going into the crate, go back to crate training at a different low-stress time. Teach going into the crate for treats and food on a cue. Then you have the cue to use when you are going to leave.

Paula Says

"I live out in the country, so when someone comes to our door, it can be quite a barking event.

Friends and relatives know to come in through the garage, so the only people coming to the front door are delivery people, service people or the occasional door-to-door salesman.

If it is someone I need to bring into the house, I send the dogs out the back door, and then let the person enter. If I am home alone, I let the dogs bark a bit behind me, almost pretending they could be a problem. Most people are intimidated and our conversations can be quite short. I even have friends who have trained their dogs to bark on a hand signal. If you are walking and someone you don't want to deal with approaches, you can pretend you don't have control of your barking dog and most people will walk away."

Chewing is a normal behavior for puppies. Direct their chewing to appropriate toys such as a Kong® filled with treats or food.

Chewing and Destructive Behaviors

Question: "Help! We just bought a purebred Labrador puppy and he is chewing up everything he can get his teeth on. If we can't get him to stop we will have to get rid of him."

Answer: The history of the puppy was he came from a breeder who raised hunting dogs. He didn't check to know whether or not the family had toddlers in the home or a fenced yard for easy access for housetraining and exercise. He also didn't ask if the family had ever owned a dog.

To be successful with a field-bred Labrador, this family will have to consider the needs of the puppy for exercise, confinement, socialization, and training. For some families this is too time-consuming and complicated and many shelters have had these high-energy pups turned in even as small puppies. Sometimes families make it through six months, hoping that neutering the dog will calm him down. When that doesn't help, hopefully they look for options like classes and play sessions.

All puppies will chew. It is normal teething and curious puppy behavior. Depending on the breed, the chewing may be less of a problem.

Our caller's puppy was scheduled into classes, the owners were coached to help with changing current behaviors and preventing other problems. This dog has gone on to be a wonderful agility competitor. The first year was definitely the toughest, so getting started early and having lots of support and coaching from class instructors and participants really helped.

Classes and Training - Attending a class specifically designed for puppies is very beneficial. Knowledgeable instructors can answer your questions.

Training is discussed in Chapter 8, but with some puppies you may want to consider specialty classes or training. If

Chewing and Destructive Behaviors *Continued*

you obtained your puppy with the intention of teaching him to hunt, learn to do agility, fly ball, or another dog sport, you may be able to find local classes that offer skills for these or other activities. You can also go online for books and DVDs that have great information. Some breeds are bred for high-level activity and will need extra training, exercise, and mental activity to help them be calm at home. Some of these breeds also need training to teach them they *can* be calm. This can be taught like a trick, literally rewarding the dog for lying down and being still.

Exercise - Even young puppies will need daily exercise in the form of walks, play time, retrieving (some retrieve naturally, some need training), and ideally, play time with both a compatible puppy and a compatible adult dog. This takes time and scheduling, but the results will be a calmer puppy who can settle down with his own toys.

Confinement - Crate training is found in Chapter 8. Crates are also handy for confining active puppies when we can't watch them. This does not mean they should be crated all day, then all night with potty breaks and a few minutes of play or training time in between. Other methods of confinement include using a leash to keep the puppy with you as you move around the house, or tether the pup to a door for a short time when you will be working near the house. Even tethered, the puppy should be supervised, and safe chew toys made available or he could start looking for options like nearby woodwork or even the feet of people within his range.

Keeping his toys interesting and rotating different ones on a daily basis will help keep his interest. Having a fenced yard just makes things a bit simpler for the family, but should not substitute for supervision outdoors for housetraining and exercise.

A Natural Aversive - Cover his favorite "off-limit" chew objects with commerical products like "Bitter Apple". Be sure to supervise puppies so they don't chew on something that will endanger them like electrical cords or socks.

Paula Says

I think puppy classes double as puppy owner therapy sessions, where owners get to see their puppy isn't the only frustrating one with issues.

They often trade tips and tricks with the other owners.

Have plenty of appropriate chew toys for your puppy. Cover his favorite "off-limit" chew objects with commerical products like "Bitter Apple". Be sure to supervise puppies so they don't chew on something that will endanger them like electrical cords or socks.

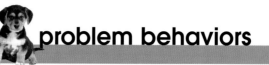
Chewing and Destructive Behaviors *Continued*

Unsafe Eating Habits

We have already established chewing is normal dog behavior.

However, when your dog begins to eat non-food items, such as clothing or rocks, this is called pica and can be dangerous to your pet.

Dogs who eat these non-food items can damage their intestines and require surgery to remove the item.

Stool-eating is a type of pica called coprophagy. Coprophagy is a behavior that is horrifying to humans but is actually instinctive and used by mother dogs to keep their den and young pups clean by eating their waste. Young pups who've seen their mother do this may be inclined to copy the behavior but usually outgrow it. If it happens with your dog, here are a few things you can try.

- Check with your veterinarian for a commercial product that can be added to your dog's food to make his stool have an aversive taste.

- Sprinkle your pet's stools, as well as any other animal's feces he may come in contact with, with Bitter Apple.

- Keep your dog on a leash, close to you on walks or whenever he is outside so you can control where he tries to wander.

- Keep your yard free of dog and cat waste.

- Do not scold or punish your dog for this behavior. Redirect his attention to another activity where you can reward him.

Socialization - Meeting lots of people, other puppies and dogs and experiencing various places is very important for a puppy. Socialization is going to prevent many problems with fear or anxiety. By the age of four months, he should be a pro at riding in a car, staying home alone, meeting strangers, especially children, being exposed to the vacuum, hair dryer, baths, having toenail trims and having his teeth and ears examined. Too often owners keep their pups home and at a later date take them out and expect them to be friendly to everyone and everything. Making up for the lack of early socialization will be much harder and take much longer.

What if your dog is destructive while you are gone?

Destructive behavior can happen because a dog is stressed due to lack of exercise or he needs more entertainment when you are gone. We get calls during the winter and after a rainy spell about dogs that are usually fine, but have become destructive. It is a good time to get creative until you can get back to the physical exercise that keeps him happy and calm.

Mental exercise can be just as tiring for the dog as physical exercise, but it takes more input from the owners. Teach new tricks, stuff Kong® toys, and hide them around the house, or look for other puppy puzzle-type toys to keep him entertained. Play retrieve for awhile before you leave for the day, or toss the ball down the stairs (if your dog is physically fit and sound) a few times to help tire him out. Take a class with him. Review the basics or look for a class that teaches something new, like agility or tricks. Seek out something fun to flex and exercise his brain. Doggy daycare is also an option.

Marking:
Inappropriate Urination

Question: "We just adopted a dog from our local shelter, a neutered male. We brought him home, and he decided to urinate all over our house. What can we do to stop this, and why is he doing it?"

Answer: Urine marking in dogs is frustrating. Many male dogs, neutered or not, and even female dogs, will urine mark.

Most dogs start marking due to stress, so going into a new home can trigger it. (Many male dogs, neutered or not and even female dogs will urine mark.) Many dogs will mark less with supervision as they settle into their new environment. Supervision and prevention is the key to success.

There seem to be specific times when some dogs mark with urine. Some mark new territory. If they are in their usual territory, some mark the same spots over and over.

Taking nearly any male dog into someone else's home can result in a marking episode, so be very careful when visiting friends and family. Keep him on a leash for a while. Keep him away from vertical surfaces in the new location and reward him for urinating outside. Take him out a bit more often than usual to try to keep his bladder empty.

With a new male dog, watch him very closely, supervise him and confine him in a crate when you can't watch him. Much like housetraining, we are encouraging marking outside but very careful to prevent it inside. Dogs mark furniture, corners, doors, and other vertical surfaces, because when things smell like the dog, it makes

him feel better. So some dogs, especially in a new location, are just trying to help their own anxiety.

Owners should encourage marking on their own property, and discourage chronic marking when on walks. A brisk pace, a pat on your leg to get his attention, and some words of encouragement to keep him moving along can help the owner control where the dog marks. He can mark on your property before you leave and when you get back but minimize marking in between.

Doggy Diapers or Belly Wraps - Some dogs have become chronic "markers" and will be very reluctant to give up what has become a habit. For these dogs, there are products called Doggy diapers or belly wraps that fit around the flanks of the male dog and cover the penis. His attempts at marking are no longer effective. This can help control marking indoors, so that everyone is calmer and the dog can have a bit of freedom around the house. Gradual reduction of indoor marking could occur as the dog starts to figure out those marking attempts inside don't work. Consistently removing the belly wrap when outdoors lets the dog successfully urinate and mark outside and gives you the opportunity to reward him there.

Occasionally there is a dog that uses feces to mark territory. You may have seen dogs who back into bushes to defecate, or can be controlling enough to drop feces occasionally along his walk. Some dogs "scratch" with front and/or back feet after urination and defecation, apparently trying to spread their scent. It seems to be a pleasurable stretching activity for some dogs, and others seem to take it very seriously.

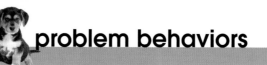

Separation Anxiety (SA)

Question: "Our dog starts to act strange when we are getting ready to leave for work. He runs from room to room barking or whining. Normally he's the perfect dog. What can we do to make him feel better about our leaving?"

Answer: Not all destructive behavior done by dogs when home alone is from SA.

Some dogs are bored, under exercised, under stimulated, and start to find behaviors that will keep themselves occupied. Burning up excess energy by chewing, barking, digging, or getting into trash or closets isn't SA.

SA is a huge emotional issue for dogs suffering from it and for clients who live with these dogs. Caring owners will turn their own lives upside down to accommodate and prevent the emotional and physical trauma for the dog.

Some generally accepted indicators of SA include:

- Growing anxiety as the owner prepares to leave the home. This may be demonstrated by pacing, trembling, whining, barking, panting, or drooling.

- Destructive behavior, often digging or chewing woodwork around or on the door that is the usual exit.

- Not eating or playing while you are gone, even if you leave specially prepared favorites.

- Urinating or defecating in the crate or in the house.

- If crated, pools of drool, damage to the crate and potential injury to the dog, especially to his paws from digging or scratching and chipped, cracked, or broken teeth from trying to break out of the crate are possible. When released from the crate the dog is often soaked with saliva, and often makes a beeline to the water dish in an effort to try to replenish his liquids.

One other trait common to some of the worst cases of SA is when the owners are home, the dog is amazing. Perfect. Never makes a mistake, and is the sweetest, calmest, nicest dog they have ever had. He loves everyone, is obedient, and perhaps most telling, he never leaves the family alone. He becomes a "Velcro® dog," one that must be touching you, lying at your feet, better yet on your feet or in your lap. If you move, he goes with you, so attentive and eager to please, yet even at this point he is probably starting to worry that you will be leaving at some point.

Separation Anxiety is relatively rare, but if a relinquished dog has SA with the previous owners, passing on that dog to someone else can be a huge trauma not only for the dog, who will probably be worse in a new environment, but also for the new owners. Owners often struggle with SA issues for months or years, not realizing there is help out there for their problems. Sometimes when we know the issues the dog had in the previous home, we can help prevent them in the next home with some instruction and tips.

SA and destructive behaviors from other causes are often mistaken for jealousy, spite, revenge, and other efforts by the dog to punish the owners. Owners might state the dog was mad at them for leaving, so he pottied in the house or tore up the remote control. The question that can help them rethink what might be going on is this: Would your dog be "bad" on purpose? Most owners think about it and reply their dog wouldn't be bad on purpose, so we can go on with our conversation to find the real problem and make an effort to help.

Relapse is common and can happen if schedules change or the family moves. If the owner gives up trying to fix the problem and passes the dog on to another home, chances are good the problem will reoccur, and possibly be worsened by the changes.

Owners who turn in dogs with SA to the shelter often casually mention the dog does not like to be alone on their information about the dog. They may hope the dog will find a home where someone is available all the time or that the dog will magically be okay in a new home. A little questioning often shows the rest of the story, and what efforts the owners tried to help the dog.

> **There are lots of ideas, theories, medications, and herbal and holistic products that claim to help with SA, but there is no single fix.**
>
> Separation Anxiety is a difficult behavior and owners must educate themselves with options to try to overcome it.
>
> I suggest you do some reading, especially Patricia McConnell's book, "I'll Be Home Soon." It is full of great suggestions for both prevention and treatment of SA. It is available at www.patriciamcconnell.com.

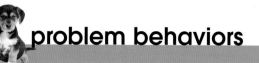

Separation Anxiety *Continued*

Some Solutions

When it comes to treating SA, working with a veterinarian with an interest in helping behavior issues is very valuable. This person can help you with potential medical issues and choosing the right medications to use along with the behavior modification program.

Following are some ideas for helping to prevent SA or working with low-level SA:

- Watch for the start of anxiety, such as when your dog knows you are leaving and starts to get worried. He may begin whining, pacing, giving anxious looks, or sometimes blocking the exit door. We want to help desensitize your exit process for the dog to help him be less anxious. Usually dogs notice when you pick up keys, put on shoes, jackets and gloves, or anything that means you are walking out the door. Practice doing these behaviors *without actually leaving* so they become less predictive or even boring to the dog.

- **Never** punish behaviors that have occurred while you were gone. You will only make your dog more anxious about your return. Walk in calmly, no matter what has occurred. That "guilty" look your dog gets is actually an attempt to calm you down, appease you and make you happy. Your dog does not connect your coming home with his previous behavior. He is reading your body language.

- Leave and come home in a very "matter of fact" manner. If possible, give your dog something interesting and fun ten or fifteen minutes before you leave, and slip out the door. Special treats, a Kong® with good stuff, or a special toy that only comes out before you leave can be good choices.

- Look for options for your dog, friends who are home during the day that will take care of him, doggy day care, or even a puppy sitter, who will come to stay with the dog during the day. While that seems like an extreme option, if your dog will do thousands of dollars worth of damage while you are gone, spending money for a pet sitter can be the economic way to go. If you are lucky enough to work in a pet-friendly office, take your dog to work. He should be friendly to strangers and okay hanging out in your office with you.

- Leave an article of clothing that smells like you with your dog when you leave.

- Work on teaching your dog it is alright to be separated from you when you are home. Teach the dog to sleep in his own bed instead of yours. Encourage him to cuddle when you ask him to, but go to another spot to hang out when you are busy in the kitchen.

One solution owners may be tempted to try is to get another dog. I worked with one family that got another dog, and it fixed the SA for their dog. That is rare, however, and most dogs who suffer from SA do not care if other dogs or cats are in the home, as it is all about the people.

What if your dog panics while in the crate and tries to break out?

This usually starts immediately after you leave. If you are crating a dog with SA, he will sometimes injure himself while trying to escape by bending bars, breaking grates, or even squeezing through tiny spaces to get out. Once out, he may be okay, or he may start on another spot with more destructive behavior. Work with a professional who is experienced. Your veterinarian will help you evaluate if certain drug therapies are in order.

Troubleshooting

Caution!

If you give up one day and decide it is too much hassle to put the dog in the crate, don't expect it to be easier the next day.

Your dog will probably think if he protests longer or harder, you will give up again, and he will continue to escalate without some real work to change his mind. Do not give up, even for one day. You want to train the behavior, so he understands and is rewarded for going into the crate many, many times.

If you are lucky enough to work in a pet-friendly office, take your dog to work. He should be friendly to strangers and okay hanging out in your office with you.

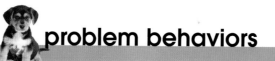
Separation Anxiety *Continued*

A Personal Story From Paula about Separation Anxiety

I did not realize the pressure Separation Anxiety puts on owners until I personally experienced it with my own dog, Tag. I adopted him with no history, as he had been turned into the shelter as a stray. A flag might have been when the Animal Control Officer commented that he barks a lot and is destructive when in the crate, but that behavior isn't uncommon. He did not mention Tag would produce huge puddles of drool if left crated, or would literally chew on the bars, chip teeth, and actually move the crate when left alone. Interestingly enough, Tag handled our shelter kennels quite well. He didn't bark or drool, seemed calm and used those spaniel eyes to attract attention.

When he didn't get adopted, my husband Wayne and I decided to adopt him and bring him home. I was surprised when the first time we left him home, not alone, but with two other dogs and two cats, we returned to a crate with bent bars, flooded with drool, and a soaked dog.

While I hadn't planned to bring him to work each day, I was fortunate to have that option. I knew leaving him home, crated or even free in the house, could be a disaster. I found a doggy day care I liked and he spent two or three days a week there. Even at work I had issues trying to leave him in my office, even if I was just outside the door. He quickly learned to open the door, and if crated, barked, and drooled extensively.

I tried the usual behavior modification program of building up time away from him gradually, changing my exit routine and giving him something amazing to do or eat when I left. Unfortunately, these things were ineffective with his level of anxiety. Frustrated, I went to talk to my veterinarian about drug therapies. He encouraged me to keep trying the behavior modifications and to add a DAP collar (Dog Appeasing Pheromone calming collar).

At about the same time, I was taking one of my other dogs to a holistic veterinarian for acupuncture treatments. She mentioned using flower essences, familiarly known as Bach Flower Essences.

My friend Robin had done some research and was able to put together a mixture of essences I could use as needed. I started using the drops along with the DAP collar, hoping to avoid going to anti-anxiety medications.

It took some months at work, having him crated with a sheet covering the crate while I was nearby. As he became more comfortable with that, I found I could come and go without a problem and I felt that we were making progress. I also found out, accidentally, when he broke out of a crate at home, that he wasn't destructive and wouldn't potty in the house if he was loose. It seemed he spent his time looking out the front bay window with its padded window seat, waiting.

We practiced with this routine, including the drops and the DAP collar for months, gradually graduating to no collar, and occasional drops. He can and will take a treat when we leave, eat it and run to the front window to watch us leave. We have come home at different times to see him asleep on the window seat. He no longer goes to doggy day care regularly, just on days he cannot come to work with me. He can be home with the other pets for several hours and does fine. It has been a gradual progression.

Puppy Nipping and Biting

Puppy mouthing and nipping is normal; it is how humans respond to it that can make the difference on whether the puppy continues, gets worse, or gradually gives it up.

Breed tendencies can make some puppies more determined to bite or nip, and herding dogs, bred to move livestock for a living can get pretty determined to use their teeth.

Caller: "We adopted Maddie, an Australian Shepherd mix at 11 weeks. The day we adopted her, she showed some aggressive tendencies in the visitation room, but I hoped it was just from the excitement of being out of her kennel and typical puppy stuff. I know now it isn't. Maddie bites constantly. Some of it just seems to be gnawing on fingers and anything else she can get in her mouth, but some of it is real anger biting. She will jump and bite, too. Our family has tried multiple tactics to get her to stop, holding her to the floor to assert dominance, subdued hold (like the vet does for exams), using a low growl ourselves and barking back at her, hand feeding. Even puppy classes didn't help. We need to break her of the biting, before she hurts someone."

Answer: **The advice you have received has not worked, and the most recent advances in training techniques *do not* advise holding her to the floor to assert dominance, growling or barking back at dogs or puppies to change their behavior.**

She could become fearful of you. Hand feeding can often help, but unless it is used in conjunction with a "Nothing in Life is Free" program, puppies can actually get worse about using their teeth, demanding food and biting to get it.

Maddie is still teething, so we can start by being certain the toys she has are helpful to her aching gums. Because cold can help, any toys that can be frozen should be in bags in the freezer. She should have access to two or three toys each day and the rest (in the freezer) are rotated out daily so each day she has something interesting to chew on. You should never use your hands to play or wrestle with her. While tug games are great for many dogs and families, until Maddie gains some control of her biting and her new teeth are all in (about six months of age), I would not recommend tugging with her.

Keep a leash on her around the house, and start teaching her some self-control by tethering her to something sturdy when she is just starting to bite. Try squeaking "ow" when she bites. Don't wait until it hurts. Some puppies will back off and be almost apologetic. If this helps, you can keep using it. If it doesn't work with your puppy, use the time out by tethering method. The first touch of her teeth gets her walked to her tie up spot and walk away. No scolding or punishment, just a couple minutes of time out.

We can teach her that using her teeth makes people leave and other types of interaction keeps people close. There will be some repetition with this technique and expect to repeat it occasionally for a few weeks. She will quickly realize that "teeth on skin" gets her isolated.

Find a trainer who can coach you using a clicker. Maddie is brilliant, probably a bit bored, and clicker training is a quick fun way to get her working for you instead of struggling against you.

Commitment

Q Caller: *We do not have a fenced yard, and we live in a high traffic area. An invisible fence is not an option for us. In mid-October our dog got loose, ran into the street, and was hit by an SUV. She is healing. Are there things we can do to modify her behavior? Please keep in mind I have young children and a husband who is not particularly fond of this dog. He stays home with the kids while I work. I realize a tired dog is a good dog, but it is hard for me to find the time to walk the dog, especially when I have children to take care of when I get home from work.*

A Paula says: *I have to start considering whether your dog is in a home that can meet her needs. I know you love her, but she needs training so she comes when called, not to mention walks, training for basic manners, and a safe place to be outdoors for potty times and play times. Please seriously consider your commitment to your dog and, as a family, decide if she is the right pet for your family. It sounds like she is great with your kids, so maybe another family with children, a fenced yard where she can play retrieve games and where they will have the time to train her would be a good decision.*

Running Away

Question: "Why do dogs run away from us?"

Answer: Many people who raise their dogs from puppies do not actually start teaching "Come" until after the puppy has figured out it can run away. The first few weeks in a new home for most puppies is spent exploring their environment, learning about their people, and getting used to the new schedule. They will usually walk or play very near their owners, and might not even think about wandering away until ten to twelve weeks. This is when, suddenly, the rest of the world is much more interesting than the world they have been living in and they will head out to explore.

Most of us will run after the puppy, calling his name or scolding him, chasing him, which is one of his favorite games. Even young puppies can run faster than most of us, so chasing becomes futile. Finally we catch the puppy, maybe scolding him for running away. We are angry, frightened he might get hurt and even disappointed that he would even consider running away from home. We need to try to think like a dog to help solve and train a recall.

Prevention is the best solution, so be sure your yard is safe. Also, work on your dog's recall (come when you are called) outlined in Chapter 8 on page 125.

The Car

One scary thing that happens occasionally after an adoption is the adopter opens his car door at home expecting his new pet to stay put while the owner gets the leash. Sometimes the dog bolts out the car door and heads down the street. Traffic, strangers, other dogs, and just plain running away is so frightening to us that we automatically launch after the dog, screaming a name the dog may not even know.

The dog may react several ways, the best one being he stops or comes back. Usually, however, the dog either enjoys the chase game or is actually frightened by the scary screaming person chasing after him and runs faster and farther.

Some solutions:

- Before you open the car door, make sure the leash is on and someone has a good grip on it so the dog can't bolt.

- Do not chase the dog. Instead make a unique noise, squeak, sound like a puppy or a kitten, and back up. If you happen to be able to grab a bag of treats, the noise the plastic bag makes can be very attractive to the dog. For some dogs jingling your keys can work.

- If you have another pet dog, put him on leash and see if the dog will come to him. Or the loose dog might come up to another dog on the street out for a walk with their owner. Hopefully he will be polite and you can apologize to the other owner and thank them if they helped catch your dog.

- If your dog loves car rides, call him in a normal voice, asking if he wants to go for a ride. Often dogs know that phrase very well and you might get him to turn back. If your dog gets far enough ahead of you, use the car to follow him, getting ahead if you safely can, then open the door and see if he will hop in.

- Use other key phrases your dog might know and like, for example, "Do you want a cookie?"

- If you need to, call Animal Control to help. They are professionals who can often help with a live trap, if necessary. If you have adopted a "special needs" dog that is especially fearful, under-socialized or even panicky, the live trap might be your best solution.

We recommend crating your dog in the car. Put a leash on him before fully opening the crate door.

Bolting Out of the House

If you have trouble with your dog bolting out a door in the house, you will want to teach a new behavior called "Wait at the Door." The dog's reward for waiting at the door is to get to go through it. You will want to work with a door your dog wants to go through, so there is a real reward for going through the door. It can be to the outdoors or there can be someone on the other side to deliver treats. Use the door to physically block the dog's way, being very careful not to let him get his nose caught as you gently shut it when he tries to go through without permission.

The Goal - Your dog sits beside you until you can fully open the door. When you are ready, you give his verbal signal (okay is often used) to go through, either ahead of you or after you have already stepped through it.

To Achieve -

Step 1: Stand at a door he wants to exit. Do not work on this when he needs to go out to go potty yet. Stand still until he sits. While he is sitting, put your hand on the doorknob.

Step 2: If he stays sitting, turn the knob.

Step 3: While he is still sitting, start to open the door an inch.

Step 4: When he gets up, which he probably will, shut the door quickly. Wait him out until he sits again, and again go through the steps to open the door an inch. When he can stay with the door open an inch, try two inches, and gradually open the door more. Each time he gets up from his sit, shut the door. This works whether the door opens toward you or away from you, but if it opens away from you, be very careful he doesn't push the door open.

If your dog gets up from his sit, shut the door. You may need to do this several times until he remains in the sit while you open the door.

Do not scold, do not give him a cue to "Sit," let him figure out that if he sits, the human will open the door. If he gets up, rushes the door, jumps on you or the door, or anything else, the door stays closed. You are literally teaching him that sitting will open the door. At some point he might wander off, so call him back to work with him more, or just try again later.

For most of our training, we end up fading or cutting back on the number of food rewards. With the recall training, I highly recommend using treats nearly all the time for training, but also using your very best treats for teaching and maintaining this exercise. On the other hand, only practice it a few times a day, five or less, so the special treats stay special.

The Yard

If your dog has learned to escape from your fenced yard, there are a couple of things to consider.

- Is he being left in the yard too long with nothing to do?

- Is he barking and causing problems with your neighbors?

- Is he digging or getting destructive out of boredom?

- Has your dog been spayed or neutered?

Owners often tell us the dog has plenty of space and lots of toys. We try to help them understand their dog knows every blade of grass and leaf in their own yard, all the toys are boring, and everything outside the fence is either really interesting (must go investigate) or scary (to be barked at).

If your fence is one of the buried electronic fences, your dog should not be outside without human supervision. While this fence may keep your dog on your property, it does nothing to keep children, dogs, or strangers off your property. Children may come onto the property to play with him, utility workers may have to intrude on the property to do their work, and your dog is left to make decisions about allowing strangers on the property with no guidance from you.

We want to approach the escaping dog with two avenues: make a better fence for him, depending on whether he goes over or under, and make his own yard more interesting.

Making a better fence.

Your neighborhood may have rules about the type of fencing you can have, however you may able to fortify it without changing the look. If your dog goes under the fence, use tent stakes to pin wire fencing to the ground. You could also use woven wire to make it very difficult for your dog to dig a hole. The woven wire is thin wire, woven in a diamond-like pattern that can be laid flat on the ground where your dog might dig. Soon it will be covered with grass and sink a bit into the soil.

If your dog goes over the fence, take a look at: www.coyoteroller.com. While this product was developed to keep coyotes out of people's yards, it works very well to keep pet dogs in, too. Some people even extend the height of their fence, which can also help.

Spay or neuter your dog

The urge to mate begins at approximately six months of age. An unneutered male dog has a natural drive to seek out female dogs. Having your dog neutered will often put a halt to his desire to escape. Females allowed to go into heat can be just as determined to find a mate. Do not let her outdoors unsupervised during this time.

Running Away *Continued*

Make the yard more interesting

Pick up all the toys and bones and put all but two away. Every day, take two toys or bones out and replace the ones he has currently, so every day he has something different to play with. Be sure to use safe toys he can't destroy or get hurt with.

Scatter favorite food or treats in the yard so your dog has to scent hunt and find all the pieces.

Take your dog's food bowl out to the yard and scatter the food in the grass. If you spray for pests or fertilize your grass, be sure to find a place safe from chemicals. Make it easy the first few days, gradually scattering the food a bit farther each meal. When he has learned to use his nose to find all the bits, scatter it farther and farther into the yard. He will not only have to "hunt" and find all the pieces, but most dogs will spend a significant amount of time retracing his steps to be sure he didn't miss any. Even scatter the food in the snow and watch him play and hunt.

If you have more than one dog, you might want to feed them one at a time, or feed one inside and the other outside. Dogs can easily become competitive for food and we do not want to start any fights.

Using a treat, teach your dog to jump through an agility "tire".

Use Kong® toys, stuffed with his meals or treats or a combination, and hide them around the yard. Be sure to subtract the amount of food fed in the toys from his daily ration of food, so you don't add extra calories to his diet.

Be interactive with him in the yard. Put together a few low jumps or obstacles. Make a ramp with a board tilted onto a step and teach him to go over or through things on a cue. You can chain several obstacles together and start a mini agility course.

Shorten the tunnel at first to make it easy for your dog.

Get a tunnel made for kids and teach your dog to follow a treat through it. Dogs love tunnels once they have gone through them a couple of times. Make the tunnel as short as possible at first, and then gradually lengthen it as he gains confidence. If your yard is a place where you and your dog have fun and interact, he will be less likely to go looking for adventures away from home.

Radio Call-ins

People Problems

Caller: *We do not own a dog, but our neighbor's dog consistently makes his "deposits" on our yard. I have tried all kinds of repellents from garden centers and natural items like red pepper flakes, but nothing works. I am not anti-dog at all. We had one, but I am finished with brown patches, broken perennials, and cleaning up messes.*

I think the people understand the problem, but they just don't care. Help!

Paula says: *Tricky question, to be sure. Short of building a fence, there isn't any simple answer, except to set boundaries with the neighbor. Even if you could catch the dog on your property, threatening the dog won't help and would antagonize the neighbor.*

Responsible dog people understand and will leash or fence their dog out of consideration. You might inquire about your community's leash laws. Likely there are laws about picking up after a dog, but that doesn't help with the urine marks.

My best suggestion is to pick up some nice bagels or cookies and take a plate to the neighbors, with the explanation that you spend lots of time and money to have your place look nice, which helps everyone's property values. Ask nicely if they would please keep their dog on their own property to potty.

Escape Artist

Caller: *We own two Brittany Spaniels, one male (neutered) and one female who is not spayed. Our female is two and has become quite the escape artist. We have a large fenced backyard and she has learned to climb the fence. We have been putting her on her tie-out for several hours after we catch her hopping the fence, and she does know she will get either kenneled or put on the tie-out after she runs away, but does not seem to mind. Other than this problem, she is a well-behaved dog. We just need to figure something out as we live in town and obviously neighbors do not like our Houdini roaming in their yards.*

Paula says: *Brittanys are a hunting breed, usually with plenty of energy to get them through a long day in the field. With this level of energy, the owners need to help the dogs beyond letting them hang out in the backyard. Dogs know every blade of grass that grows there and are quickly bored. Add to boredom the ability to climb or jump fences, and the dog goes looking for adventure.*

Follow-up: *We added scatter feeding in the yard, rotating that with stuffed Kongs® and large meaty raw bones (check with your veterinarian before giving your dogs bones, but if you do, they should always be raw). The owners modified the fence, using a product similar to the one sold on www.coyoteroller.com. I also recommended spaying this female dog, since the drive to reproduce can cause her to escape and wander or can bring male dogs to their property, exposing their dogs to fights or disease.*

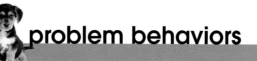
Thunderstorm Phobias

Q Caller: *I adopted a wonderful Cockapoo, Hannah, at age one. She transitioned so well into her new home, where we lived from October to May of the next year. She has never been bothered by storms. After our move to a new home, however, she has become so frightened of thunder and lightning. She wakes me up and shakes and shakes until she falls back to sleep or the storm stops. I am, of course, tormented as to what she must do if there is a storm when I am gone.*

Plus, with July 4th coming, I fear she will panic when the fireworks start. She is otherwise perfectly docile and independent.

A Paula says: *Because you got her as a young dog before winter, I am guessing she had never noticed storms before. When the summer storm season started, she took notice. I am not saying to ignore the dog, but don't baby her either. Instead, be pretty matter of fact. Bring out the good treats, and consider Melatonin, an over-the-counter product which can be useful for calming some dogs, and you can give it even after the storm has started.*

It is hard to know why some dogs get scared. Even in the same home setting, one dog might become frightened, and another will ignore the storm.

Thunderstorms, Fireworks, and Other Phobias

Question: "Our white German Shepherd has no fear when it comes to protecting our livestock from predators, but when a thunderstorm starts he races for the house. Once inside he hides behind the furnace in the basement. Is there anything we can do to help him feel better?"

Answer: Every July we get phone calls from owners with dogs that panic due to fireworks being set off. Sometimes you see proud pet owners take their pets along to the fireworks display, and some of the dogs seem to do fine. That is great, but so many dogs learn to be fearful of sudden explosive sounds that we can't help but believe some are traumatized. Other things dogs can be very fearful of include camera flashes, vacuums, motorcycles, gunshots, and thunderstorms.

Some dogs go to a special place during storms. Here, Pip "hides" under a table.

Thunderstorms, Fireworks, and Other Phobias *Continued*

Thunderstorms are a bit different than other noises because the environment changes and makes the thunderstorm somewhat predictable for the dog. He may see the clouds coming in, feel the barometric changes, or be able to hear the thunder a long time before we can. Dogs may start to pace, drool, try to find a place to hide, or try to break into or out of the house. Dogs have gone through windows and doors, broken out of crates, crawled under beds, and hidden in showers or bathtubs.

Phobias can be inadvertently heightened by owners who are too sympathetic in their behaviors with the dog. Be nice and very matter of fact, but don't act like there is something wrong. Go about your regular business as best as you can.

> ## Read through the website:
> www.lindatellington-jones.com to learn about her techniques for calming and training dogs called TTouch.
>
> With a little bit of training and practice, her techniques can work wonders on fearful pets.

Try some of the suggestions listed below to see if they help your dog.

- Ask your veterinarian about trying Melatonin. This is a product sold over the counter, marketed for humans and available anywhere that sells vitamins. There do not appear to be any side effects with dogs and we have used it for years with fearful and stressed shelter dogs. Dogs that are having a hard time with panic can get one dose two or three times a day for three to four days, but often, even after the first dose, you will see the dog starting to get calmer. We have had success with dogs with storm phobias doing better after using it for a few storms in a row. Even if you get home and the dog is already afraid, try giving the melatonin. Hopefully you will see the dog start to act more like he does when the storm passes—breathing normally, acting less frantic, maybe even able to eat or take a treat.

- You can purchase DVD's with many sounds on them that can be used to help desensitize your dog to noises. Start by playing the sound very low, and if your dog doesn't seem to notice the sound, practice sit or other behaviors he knows well, using great treats and a happy tone of voice. Very gradually increase the sound level, playing with your dog at each change. When your dog starts to notice the sound, see if he will keep working and overcome his concern. If at any point he becomes stressed, lower the sound level to a comfortable point and work with him again. Use several sessions for this work. See if he can be more comfortable during the next storm, when you vacuum or when there are fireworks.

- Giving treats during a storm won't work for most dogs, but if you can distract him at the beginning of his reaction, you may be able to lessen it. If he loves toys, stuffed squeaky toys, or has a favorite food, see if you can get him interested in these things as early in the storm as possible. Early rather than in the middle is when you might have the best chance to minimize his reaction.

Thunderstorms, Fireworks, and Other Phobias *Continued*

Your dog should have a place to hide where he feels safe.

- Create a safe place for your dog to hide. Take note of where he goes when frightened and make sure he has access to that space.

- DAP (dog appeasing pheromone) is a calming scent for dogs and could be helpful. It comes as a spray to use "as needed," a collar the dog wears all the time, or as a wall plug-in diffuser. The idea is to have the product floating around the dog's head so it can mimic the calming effect his mother's pheromones had when he was young.

- Other ideas people have tried include acupuncture with a certified veterinary acupuncturist; homeopathic preparations, some herb preparations, and as a last resort, an anti-anxiety type of medication prescribed by your veterinarian. Extreme phobias can get a dog in big trouble, so try some of these ideas first. However, if you just can't get him calmed down enough to be safe, talk to your veterinarian about a prescribed medication.

- A "Thundershirt" is a fabric jacket the dog wears. The theory behind the jacket is you are calming the nervous system which has a calming effect on the dog. Several pet owners relate their positive experiences with it. It can be used for other problems like Separation Anxiety, travel fears, barking and other fears. The website www.thundershirt.com has a lot of great information.

Many dog owners say putting a "Thundershirt" on their dog has a calming effect. Several similar products are on the market.

Chasing, Herding, and Jumping on Children

Question: "We have a big fenced yard, three children, and a one-year-old Collie. The kids get frustrated, because every time they start to run, wrestle, or chase a ball, the dog gets in the way, trips them, or starts barking and nipping at them. We adore Sheba, and while we know she is supposed to herd sheep, how can we keep her from chasing our kids?"

Answer: Sheba is genetically predisposed to herd sheep. So, without sheep, Sheba will then transfer her genetic drive to whatever will work, and that will be your children. Some dogs will also herd other dogs, cats, even leaves. While it can be a great talent if she is a working dog on a farm or a competitor in herding contests, as a pet, it can be an annoying and even painful behavior for your children.

We want to teach Sheba to channel her herding drive into other activities. Retrieving toys or balls with her can help. Be sure she knows basic good manners, like Sit, Lie Down, or Stay. Encourage the kids to teach her some fun tricks they can show off to their friends.

When the kids want to play tag, or games that involve running and playing in the yard, use a few of the toys Sheba loves. Put them on leashes or light ropes, or on the end of a fishing pole and have the kids drag them behind them or off to the side of where they are running. There are toys on the market, already on a pole, that are meant for this game. Sheba will likely chase the toys instead of the kids. The kids should let Sheba "catch" the toys once in a while, but they will all enjoy this game much more than the one where she tries to turn them into sheep.

Another idea is to teach the children to get a special treat or bone for Sheba, put her in her crate, and let her have something great so they can play outdoors without her. Don't do this all the time, but it could be a part of her day or in addition to playing with the dragged toy.

Encourage the kids to set up some obstacles and teach Sheba to go over and through them. It can be as simple as draping a tarp over a clothes line to make a tunnel, setting up some poles or broomsticks on some blocks for jumps.

If she is jumping on the kids to get attention and trying to get them to run or play, teach the kids to "freeze" until she stops. Being consistent with this will help teach Sheba that jumping up doesn't work. Reward her for sitting or any appropriate activity.

If she is using her teeth to get attention or seems to be escalating even with training and exercise, please contact a behavior professional to help work through this problem.

This family did a great job modifying Sheba's herding behavior, enrolled her in basic training classes, and also went on to agility classes.

Training a Puppy to Chase a Toy

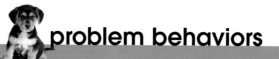
Growling, Whining, and Other Verbalization

Dog Play

Question: "Our dogs Whiskey and Bourbon are playing, at least we think so, but our concern is the amount of growling and snarling they do with each other. They are very noisy. They stop when we call them and there is never any injury or blood. We are concerned about the noise and worry it will get out of hand and they will hurt each other. Should we stop them?"

Answer: The dogs' history is they are neutered male Boxer mixes, not related but about the same age. Whiskey was the first dog, and Bourbon came a few months later. They were best buddies right away. They have been playing like this for several years, and the play sessions happen several times a day. They seldom play with toys, separately or together. Whiskey seems to be the rougher player, and sometimes Bourbon will crouch and freeze or will try to hide under a table, appearing to want to get away from Whiskey. But as soon as the owners call him or tie up Whiskey, Bourbon is back pestering him to play again. So it is possible that while Whiskey seems to be the rougher dog, Bourbon could be the instigator that actually starts the rough play.

Without actually seeing the dogs play, and with their history of noise but no injury or escalation to actual biting, we would encourage the owners to work with them on a couple things.

- Interrupt the play sessions every few minutes. Chances are good they are doing some short "breathers" already, but owners do not always notice. Having the owners set the tone for the play helps give the dogs some boundaries. When you interrupt them, call them away from each other, but **don't drag them apart**. Reward each dog separately with a treat or good rub-down or scratch, and then let them go back to playing. Timeouts should be five to twenty seconds, very short but long enough to bring the excitement level down.

- Be sure the dogs have other activities and this is not their only exercise. Some activities should be done separately. Perhaps each dog gets walked by himself sometimes. We would encourage the owners to give bones or special treats separately, so the dogs never start to guard from each other. Playing retrieve or teaching manners or tricks should be done separately but at the same pace with each dog, if possible.

- Watch for play sessions that get especially loud, or where one dog seems to be trying to leave or hide. **Do not punish the dog that appears to be bullying him**, but do separate them for a few minutes. One dog may be stressed, anxious, or aroused by something else in the environment. His reaction to outside stressors can cause him to play rougher than normal.

Growling, Whining, and Other Verbalization *Continued*

- Quick calm intervention by the owners can help bring both dogs back to their regular play level. Letting them work it out for themselves can sometimes cause more harm by letting the aroused dog escalate. One dog escalates, and the other dog becomes frightened. The scared dog may start to show aggressive but defensive behaviors to try to get the other to back off. Suddenly we have a dog fight for real, with both dogs extremely aroused and frightened owners who have to decide what to do. When we get to this point, it can be difficult to get the dogs to "play nice" with each other. In some cases, one dog must leave the home permanently, so prevention and supervision are very important.

Use a treat to interrupt a play session and bring down the excitement level.

The result was that these owners decided to work with both dogs separately, taking them to classes, on walks and training separately, so that when the dogs were together, the same cue would work for both dogs. Supervised play was allowed with lots of interruptions and as the dogs got older and a bit less active, the play modified into a less rowdy and more acceptable form.

Some verbal communication between dogs can sound very serious to us, but is actually playing for the dogs. Some dogs always play "noisy", some always play "quiet" and some dogs will adapt their play style according to what the other dog does or prefers. It is fun watching dogs that are flexible enough to adapt their play styles to their new friends. Larger dogs can learn to play gently with puppies or small adult dogs. Tiny dogs may be able to communicate enough to be safe around large dogs but their play should always be supervised.

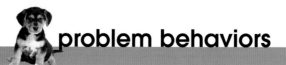
Growling, Whining, and Other Verbalization *Continued*

Growling

Growls can be territorial, fearful, or a warning of rough or dangerous behavior by another dog, child, adult, or other pet and care should be taken to determine why the dog chose to growl. Growling does not mean the dog's next move is to bite. It is one level of communication the dog gives us.

If you hear a low, throaty growl from your dog or any dog, it is a sound to take seriously, especially if the growl is happening at the same time as a frozen body position. Our human nature tells us to punish this growl, whether it is aimed at us, another dog or animal, or a stranger. This growl is a communication by your dog and we need to find out why he is growling. If we punish this noise, we may teach the dog not to growl, but it doesn't mean the reason for the growl is gone. Because he is still aroused or stressed but has been taught not to growl, he may feel he has to escalate his behavior to get his point across, and that can turn into lunging, barking, snapping, snarling, and biting.

Since we don't want those behaviors either, try to determine why the dog is growling. Is he in pain, stressed, frightened but trapped and can't move away? Is he being "attacked" by a puppy who doesn't know any better, and he is growling to try to teach him some manners and to honor an adult dog?

If this is a stray or neighborhood dog growling at you and you feel the hair on the back of your neck stand up, trust yourself that this is a bad situation and look for options. Usually, if you stand very still, he may sniff you, even mark on you but will decide you are no threat and not interesting and move on. If you move, chances are good he will chase and possibly bite you.

Do not try to 'stare down' the dog or scream and wave your arms around to get him to go away. These things will only increase the dog's agitation.

Whining

Whining is a noise dogs make for various reasons, but most often it is to seek attention. It starts in the nest with their mother, with the pups whining and making similar sounds that encourage the mother to let them nurse. Puppies often start whining at their new families to get attention for cuddle time, feeding, or play time. If you respond to the puppy each time, talking to him, feeding or playing with him when he whines, you are teaching him you will respond to his whining.

Many owners go along with this for awhile. But as the puppy gets bigger and is jumping higher and whining or barking louder and in a more demanding way, he must learn to use some self-control. When a behavior is attention-seeking, any time we scold it, or respond to it in any way, we are reinforcing the behavior and it will continue. Teach the puppy a different behavior that will work to get attention. Sit is a behavior the puppy can learn quickly and be rewarded for.

Howling

Some dogs howl for music or something they hear on TV. Some howl because of sirens, and some have been taught to howl on a cue from their owners, which usually involves the owner howling to get them started.

Some breeds howl more than others, like Siberian Huskies and mixes and Alaskan Malamutes. When we have a dog that howls at the shelter, you can sometimes hear whole rooms of dogs start to join in. That can raise the hair on the back of your neck, to say the least.

Wolves apparently use howling as part of their communication system, but we think most dogs use it as a stress release.

Baying

Baying is a breed-specific sound that some hounds make instead of or in addition to barking. Bloodhounds, Coon Hounds, Beagles, and Basset Hounds are known to bay, and it seems that people either love it or hate it.

Barkless Dogs

Some breeds of dogs, such as the Basenji, have been marketed as "barkless" and it does appear they do not bark, but they do have a huge vocabulary including yodels, yips, whines, and howls. Barkless doesn't necessarily mean quiet. As always, do your research before deciding to add a dog to your family.

Some happy endings
from the Animal Rescue League of Iowa

Hailey

My Hanging Tree Cow Dog mix Hailey was surrendered by her previous owner to ARL at around 4 months of age. ARL contacted Protege Canine Rescue about finding the right home for her. Protege specializes in finding homes for overly active dogs that might be hard to place in an everyday home. I am a foster home for Protege rescue and Hailey was placed with me. After several weeks with Hailey, it was clear I would not be able to give her up. We had an immediate connection and a strong friendship.

I began training Hailey to play flyball with Skidmarkz, a local club. Hailey showed great potential and clearly enjoyed herself. She ran in her first tournament in August 2010 and did great! Soon after, Hailey started rapidly dropping weight and was spending her time throwing up. She went from from 35 to 23 pounds in two months. After months of vet visits and testing, it was discovered Hailey has a disease called EPI (Exocrine Pancreatic Insufficiency), which means she is unable to digest any food. After several more months of trying different medications and food testing, I was able to find the right mix and Hailey is back up to 32 pounds.

In March 2011 Hailey was able to compete in her first flyball tournament since her diagnosis and ran on Skidmarkz's A team with some smoking times as low as 4.4 seconds! Jayne McQuillen, Skidmarkz flyball team and my mother, Jo Pearson, have all been incredibly supportive and helpful. Everyone knew what a great dog Hailey was and how much I loved her. Because of ARL's devotion to save dogs and place them in the right home, Hailey has found a happy place to enjoy good friends for the rest of her life.

Emily

Gone to a Good Home!

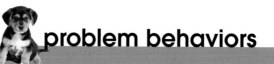
Jumping Up

Jumping up is a greeting behavior many dogs will use to get closer to our faces.

They may also use it to get attention, as in the case of smaller dogs. Dogs will stand on their back legs with front paws extended on your torso or scratching at your body or arms, or wrapped around you like they are hugging you.

The problem is it can be uncomfortable, damage clothing, may cause injury to adults or children, and toenail scratches can do serious skin damage to older people. While this is a normal greeting behavior for dogs, it should be considered a behavior not allowed unless on a cue. Many dogs, especially small dogs, jump up to get attention or to get a "lift" into your arms. The same technique we use for the big dogs that jump up will work quickly and effectively for small dogs. As with any training or behavior modification, consistency is vital and all members of the household should agree to the changes. If one member of the household encourages the dog to jump up, the training will be inconsistent and frustrating.

To stop the behavior, begin by teaching the dog to Sit on a hand signal or verbal cue. Use the signal BEFORE the dog starts to jump on you, family members, or a guest. Be sure to coach everyone that no one talks to, pets, or makes eye contact with the dog until he sits. Proof it and practice it a lot, especially at the door where visitors enter.

You should practice when there are no visitors, then practice when a family member enters. You may want to start with the dog on a leash so you can keep him in the area or walk away with him if he gets too excited. Finally, ask a good friend to help you change your dog's behavior and practice with them. Be prepared to reward liberally with treats, praise, and attention from the visitor, when the dog is successful.

The dog's history can make a difference, so if he has been jumping up to greet for five years, it could take a little more training for him to learn to change his behavior to get attention and rewards.

What Not To Do

We do not ever want to punish the dog for jumping on someone.

Punishment can result in the dog blaming or being resentful of the person he was greeting. We want him to always enjoy greeting people. We just want him to be appropriate.

- Practice when you are walking your dog. Ask him to sit to greet anyone on the walk, even if the person is just walking by. Practice this consistently so he is polite and well-mannered if someone wants to visit.

- Many people step on their dog's back toes or hold their paws or knee the dog in the chest. **These "fixes" do not work.** They give the dog the attention he wants. In some cases, a knee in the chest has broken a dog's ribs. Holding a dog's paws can make him "paw shy". Modify the behavior by teaching a SIT. He can't jump if he is sitting.

Training FOUR
ON THE FLOOR

Stealing and Guarding

Question: "My adopted shelter dog, Ozzie, is part Great Pyrenees and a wonderful sweetheart giant of a dog. Lately he has stopped eating his food and started stealing bread and other goodies from my kitchen counters."

Answer: This was a new behavior that coincided with his reluctance to eat his dog food. A sudden change in behavior often indicates a medical issue, so we recommended she consult with her veterinarian.

We also suggested she change to a brand of dog food that didn't contain grains. We suspected the food Ozzie was eating wasn't agreeing with him, and most dogs will quickly become reluctant to eat a food that makes them uncomfortable or nauseous. But once he stopped eating his food, he was hungry so started looking for something to eat. The owner had never had him steal off the counters before and when he would steal and eat a whole loaf of bread, she was stunned. She found a food he liked, and the counter surfing stopped. Because Ozzie just plain liked bread, she did have to be careful to keep it out of reach for a few week. But because he was no longer hungry, he wasn't hunting.

Ozzie's owner was happy to report success with the new food. She was thrilled he loved the new food and equally thrilled he wasn't counter surfing anymore.

Dog Tales

My friend Suzanne has a Border Collie, Bree (smart and agile). One Christmas season Suzanne was baking her special bread filled with cream cheese. Six loaves were cooling on the kitchen island. She was in another part of the house, and when she came back to the kitchen, only five loaves remained. No crumbs, no paw prints, and it was the loaf in the middle that had disappeared. Since Bree couldn't have stolen the loaf without leaving some sign, she asked her husband if he had eaten one. He denied it, too, and to this day she doesn't understand why Bree took the middle loaf, and how she didn't leave any telltale signs of her golden opportunity.

A plastic carpet runner, with the nub side up, makes an unpleasant landing spot for a dog that likes to counter surf.

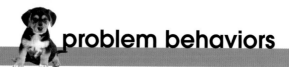

Stealing and Guarding *Continued*

Stealing

Dogs are born thieves. That is not a bad behavior; it is a genetic drive that allows dogs to survive if food is scarce. Some dogs are born polite and wouldn't take a chicken wing off your plate if you left it on the floor. Most, however, would take it without any hesitation.

Because it is such a normal behavior for dogs, we have to train them to try to keep it under our control. We also need to train ourselves and our family members to put food away, so there is less opportunity. A great training method to help with stealing is to teach Leave It as described in Chapter 8, but that also means you need to be present when the temptation arises. It is unfair to expect a dog to leave a yummy opportunity if you aren't there to supervise. Fortunately, most pet dogs don't jump on counters or tables to steal food.

Solutions

You can try "booby traps" for persistent counter surfing dogs. Examples might be putting eight to ten pennies into about a dozen empty pop cans, and taping them shut. Arrange a sheet of newspaper on your dog's favorite counter and stack the cans a few inches from the edge but on the newspaper. Since your dog will put his paws on the counter first to look for goodies, he will shake the newspaper and all the cans will fall down, becoming an unpleasant experience for him.

You can also try double-stick tape on the edge of the counter; many dogs hate the feel of it on their feet. Punishing or scolding the dog yourself is not very effective, as he will just learn to counter surf when you are not in the room.

Prevention is the best solution. However, be sure there is nothing on the counters your dog will be interested in. This includes dirty plates, pans, or cookie sheets, any food products, and anything with food in it.

"Manners Minder"

A "Manners Minder" is a great training tool.

It is a treat delivery machine you can set up to deliver treats without having to be present.

For example you can train a down-stay. Your dog gets treats randomly from the machine for lying on his bed.

Training LEAVE IT with an Untrained Dog

Stealing and Guarding *Continued*

You might also want to teach your dog the only spot in the kitchen he is allowed to be is in his dog bed in the corner. All treats are placed in that spot and a few days of training, using his food or treats will help him stay reliably in his spot, instead of underfoot.

Guarding

Another issue many multi-dog households have is dogs who guard their food, bones, or toys from the other dogs in the family. This is a tricky behavior to change because we do not want to punish or scold the dog that guards, as it could lead to more guarding if he thinks the other dogs got him in trouble. Instead, management is a good way to control this.

The guarding dog only gets his special treasures in his crate or in a separate room and they are picked up the rest of the time. Another option that can work for some dogs is to get lots of the same toy or bones, at least twice as many as there are dogs. Then it becomes difficult for the guarder to hoard them all, plus they are no longer special, because there are many.

If your dog guards his food bowl, treats, toys, or bones from you or any human you will want to get help from a behavior professional to manage and modify this behavior. Working on Leave It and Want to Trade in Chapter 8 will help, but more can and should be done to help the dog be as safe in your home as possible.

You can also use the food bowl to train your dog not to guard. Feed him bits of food by hand from the food bowl as you lower it. Never pick the food bowl back up during this training. Once you give it to the dog, allow him to eat.

Start right away using a food bowl to teach your dog not to guard his food.

Training with the Food Bowl

Training a Dog to TRADE

Some happy endings
from the Animal Rescue League of Iowa

Sam

Things have been GREAT since we adopted Sam! He is truly a special dog. From day one he has been just a perfect fit in our home. He has an amazing personality and is so smart. We have had no issues whatsoever. We are truly thankful we have been given the opportunity to have him in our lives. We are even more thankful that Heartland Weimaraner Rescue was able to step in and and provide a home until he could come to us. You did an amazing job! I know nothing about the ARL but am glad they were able to take good care of him until you took over. This is truly a success story in so many ways. First, Sam was able to go from shelter to rescue and have another chance at finding a permanent home. Unfortunately, as you know that isn't always the case. Second, he is six- years-old and some families would rather have a puppy or a young dog. While that is great, I feel many people miss out on having a wonderful companion like Sam by not giving an older dog a chance.

I use the term "old" lightly as he has PLENTY of spunk. He truly has a place in our hearts and is a happy dog.

Thank you again for the work that you have done and also thanks to the shelter for starting the process.

Patrick

Aggressive Behavior Reactions to Dogs or People

We want to remind you that aggressive behavior is behavior.

It is behavior that became part of the dog's life for some reason, sometimes we never know why. All behavior can change, but it will not change for the better without help from his humans. Dogs don't grow out of or spontaneously recover from whatever caused them to start behaving aggressively.

Many times we get calls from owners who have worried about a behavior their dog does for a long time, sometimes years, hoping or assuming it would get better and he would "grow out of it." Now the dog has had all that time to try to work out his own concerns, practicing aggressive behavior over and over.

Get help early on if you suspect a problem. Attend basic classes with a positive trainer, teaching some behaviors and increasing your communication with your dog.

Why do dogs use aggressive behavior?

The simple reason is because it works.

Almost all aggressive behavior dogs use is based in fear. It is pretty rare that dogs raised as pets fight, bite, or have any antagonistic or combative reaction that is not based in fear. Dogs learn quickly that proactive behavior, including growling, hackles raised, showing teeth, eyes wide and staring, barking, lunging, and biting will make a scary "thing" go away. It is a coping mechanism dogs may feel forced to use when they are unable to use the "flight" part of "fight or flight."

Aggressive Behavior Reactions to Dogs or People *Continued*

"Fight or Flight" are the generally accepted options dogs may have in situations of confrontation. A third option we sometimes see from dogs in stressful or confrontational situations is something we call "flirt." For example, dog meets a dog, and instead of either dog leaving or starting a confrontation, one dog finds something to play with and diverts the attention of the other dog into a game. Dogs also do this with people. If someone speaks harshly to them, or even if owners are having a loud discussion on any topic, the dog or puppy may grab a toy and try to start a game.

Dogs can get very creative, sometimes even pretending to have a toy, or just using play bows, happy face, and submissive behaviors to interest the other dog or person into a game. For most dogs, the goal is to prevent any sort of conflict.

Some dogs have what is referred to as "global" fear, and seem to be afraid of their environment and their owners, as well as any thing or any place new. These dogs have usually been poorly socialized when young and sometimes are products of a genetic mix that may contribute to these issues.

Often, despite the owner's best efforts, these dogs live miserable, anxiety-filled lives. Sometimes behavior modification and drug therapy can help to make them comfortable, but seldom will these dogs become "normal" dogs able to go in public, meet people normally, and play with other dogs.

There are some dogs that seem to be born ready to use their teeth to get their way. We see these puppies occasionally at the shelter. These are the pups you pick up and they growl, show

Dog Tales

Suzanne had a Border Collie that seemed to have been born with extreme fear he chose to show as aggressive behavior. From the time she got him at ten weeks old, the beautiful blue merle, blue-eyed Border Collie would bite her, didn't enjoy handling, and was terrified of nearly any person or dog. She thought she had done her research well, finding a responsible breeder who would choose the right puppy from her latest litter for Suzanne's goals. Bleu was so fearful, his every choice was to growl, snarl, or bite.

I never knew why she didn't give up on this dog, but she did her very best, modifying and managing his behavior and working with many trainers. She was always looking for the magic "key" that would help Bleu lose his fear and become the dog she knew he wanted to be. Drug therapy did help, years of training and behavior modification did help, and Bleu did have several dog friends and human friends he did well with. His life was cut short by a very aggressive cancer, but Bleu taught us all so much in his life. We called him an honorary shelter dog, because if he had gone to anyone but Suzanne, he would have landed in a shelter, getting adopted because of his looks and returned because of his behavior.

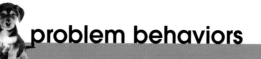
Aggressive Behavior Reactions to Dogs or People *Continued*

their teeth, and look at you with a hard stare. You try to pet them and they growl, try to bite, squirm, struggle, and threaten. You give them a toy and start to take it away, and they threaten or attack, ready to bite.

The breed of the dog isn't a factor, as we have seen this personality type in nearly every breed. It seems to be something genetic, born into the dog, not learned. They are not feral or wild, they just don't enjoy or need human contact.

Biting Behavior

We encourage any owner with a dog who has threatened to bite or has bitten a human or another pet to find a behavior professional to help try to modify the dog's behavior.

Working on this by yourself is difficult and can be quite dangerous. Do not try what you may have seen on TV or what your neighbor or co-worker recommends. Do not try to find a new home for a dog that threatens or bites humans or pets, as it is not fair to the next family, no matter what information you give them. It is also not fair to your dog.

If you cannot safely modify your dog's behavior, discuss your options with your veterinarian. From our point of view, if you turn this dog into an animal shelter with full disclosure of his problems, you should expect the shelter to take the responsible step of euthanizing this dog. Shelters need to make a responsible decision about the potential for damage or injury to the next adopter, if serious behavior issues are known.

Sometimes before we evaluate the puppies, we are amazed they are at the shelter, so cute and young, what could have happened that the owner couldn't or wouldn't keep this puppy? When we find these threatening behaviors and can rule out the puppy has fear, we understand completely why the average pet owner didn't keep this puppy, as they can be very scary.

Fear Issues

Two main fear issues that are common topics for client consultations are: dogs who are afraid of strangers and dogs who are afraid and reactive to other dogs. Some dogs have both issues, and that is an especially difficult project. Each of these issues can take time, sometimes even years of work, depending on the owner's goals for the dog.

Dogs Afraid of Strangers

Since we know a dog will sit because he has been rewarded for the behavior previously, growling or any other aggressive behavior must similarly have been rewarded, at least in the mind of the dog, or he would not continue to use it. So if the first time a dog growls at a stranger, and the stranger leaves, the dog has been rewarded. If the first time a dog barks at the letter carrier delivering mail, the letter carrier leaves, the dog is rewarded.

If we yell or scold the dog, he may also think we are backing him up or barking along with him. He may interpret the punishment to mean the presence of the stranger or letter carrier causes him problems, so, yes, they are still scary. It is very easy for punishment to be misinterpreted by the dog, and it is a major reason to stop using it as a training tool.

Dog Tales

Children/Family Aggression Issues

Jake is a two-year-old neutered male Rat Terrier. The Johnsons got him as a puppy and did some training with him when he was younger. After attending a puppy class, they let the training slide. He began to look and sound aggressive with other dogs on walks.

They were especially concerned their son Michael, age seven, was at risk. As Jake was looking out the window, with Michael standing nearby, Jake growled at Michael. I always want parents to put their children first if the dog is having problems, but with some supervision, education, and encouragement, most families can work things out.

I suggested the Johnsons consider Good Manners training classes at the shelter. Also, it seemed wise to suggest they carry treats on walks, change directions as needed to keep his attention on them, not on the environment. If he looks at or toward a dog but doesn't react, he gets a big reward for that.

When the family walks Jake they can play "look at that," a game with any object, in which they give Jake the chance to look at something, and then look back at the owner for a reward. For example, when Michael moves or makes a noise and Jake looks toward him, they can wait until he looks back at them and then quickly reward the "looking back" part so he starts to understand it is not about looking away from them. The reward comes for looking back at them.

Also, for training, I suggested they use a Gentle Leader™ head collar, a clicker, such as iClicks, or even a pen, and read a book called Click to Calm by Emma Parsons. When they go on walks, Michael clicks, and one of the Johnsons gives treats. Jake is slowly learning to look at both of them. They also have signed up for classes.

Notes on this case: Jake likely will never hang out with other dogs in a group. However, he can learn to walk calmly with his family in their neighborhood. Since success may seem to come slowly, I suggest families keep a journal to help them remember their progress.

Also, to help sweeten the relationship, I suggested the Johnsons put Michael in charge of Jake's food, with direct supervision from them. Having Michael feed Jake, while asking Jake to perform for each bite, gives Michael credibility. Suddenly Michael is important to Jake. He must listen to Michael or go hungry.

> ### Reactive dogs won't be "cured" but can be managed and their behavior modified to the point other people may not even know there is a problem.
>
> Some dogs can be socialized and taught dog language to help them communicate with other dogs more normally.

Prevention

To begin working on any behavior problem with our dogs, start with the "Nothing In Life is Free" protocol in Chapter 8 . We want our dogs to be assured we will make all decisions they may need, especially when the big questions come along. When we meet a dog on the street, your dog should be checking in with you, not staring down the other dog. When a stranger comes to your home, your dog should be responding to your cues to sit so the stranger can enter and meet the dog in a mannerly way.

If your dog is fearful of strangers that come into your home, make the decision about any interaction the dog and the stranger may have—whether your dog meets the stranger, how that meeting is handled, and where the dog will be during the visit and when the visitor is ready to leave. None of this involves punishment for the dog, and by using some of the following tips, you may prevent many problems with your dog.

Dogs Who Are Reactive to Other Dogs

This behavior is usually much worse on a leash than when the dog is loose. Our client dog exhibits lunging and barking at the other dog while on walks. A few dogs not only do that but might also threaten the owner out of frustration by biting the leash or even the owner himself, struggling to get to the other dog. This can be a serious escalation of aggressive behavior and dangerous to the handler, so you should seek professional help if your dog starts redirecting his frustration on you or other objects, people, or pets.

Dogs tend to greet each other more naturally when they are not on a leash.

We always ask if the dog has any Doggy buddies. Usually there are one or two dogs he will get along with. Maybe he met them when he was young, or lives with or next to a dog he gets along with. It is the strange dog he meets or sees on the streets that causes the reaction.

Aggressive Behavior Reactions to Dogs or People *Continued*

Why would dogs dislike other dogs? It can start on the street with a large stray that rushes up to you and your dog and scares you both. Now your dog fears large dogs. Maybe he meets a dog at the dog park that is brown and who plays too rough and scares your dog. Now he doesn't like brown dogs either. When his efforts to stay away from them don't work, he tries facing off with them, barking, and snarling. They leave. He has learned a new behavior.

From here, your dog may start to generalize that all loose dogs are scary. Eventually, all dogs, loose or on leash are scary. Even if we do know why the dog is reactive, the treatment will be the same.

This can be a very tough process because the variety of scenarios for this behavior differs with each dog.

Success depends on the owners. Our tendency with a dog that barks, growls, or lunges at other dogs is to punish him, pull back on the leash and we often become very tense ourselves, actually mirroring the behavior of the dog. He may think we "agree" with him, are backing him up and his behavior will often escalate if we react this way. So part of the training is literally coaching the owner about his role— calm, quiet voice tones, calm but not still or frozen body language, and, of course, keep breathing. When the dog is stressed, owners tend to stop breathing, get very still, and shout at their dog.

Punishment will not help reactive behavior. Punishing the dog for his fears make his fears worse and now, you as his owner, have become useless to him for backup, defense or any other options. Do not use scolding, leash jerking, or harsh collars. Instead, train your dog for appropriate behaviors.

CAUTION

We suggest getting a trainer with experience to help you.

If your dog has ever threatened you, bitten you or bitten another human or pet, you must find a professional to help.

It is just not safe to work with the dog on your own.

Aggressive Behavior Reactions to Dogs or People *Continued*

Dog Tales

Our chocolate Labrador, Shady, passed away quietly at home. She had come to live with us after our neighbors divorced and neither one could have her. She had run loose out in the country with their older Labrador for several years, fence fighting with our dogs (who were safely inside our fence). I always thought if all the dogs met outside of the fence they would not get along because of all the years of frustration and barking they had done.

When Shady came to live with us, we first considered finding her a new home, but I quickly found some behaviors that concerned me enough to decide to keep her. The last thing I wanted was for Shady to get adopted, be unsuccessful in her new home, and be returned. So for a month or so she basically lived in a separate part of our house, being able to see and sniff our dogs occasionally but not participating as a household member.

One day my husband let her into the house while I was gone. She did fine—fine with the dogs, fine with the cats. Well, she did not want the cats too close and gave a nice warning bark at them. I soon found out that with strange dogs, she was afraid and would do the same warning growl/bark. She would show her teeth, give us lots of warning, but wanted nothing to do with playing or being around strange dogs.

I started attending classes with Shady, teaching her to check in with me, look at the other dogs and check back with me, and to tolerate casual contact with other dogs. She did a great job of learning the basics, had several tricks she was good at, and loved some basic agility obstacles.

Suggestions:

Our goal is to walk nicely in public on a leash where other dogs are in sight without barking or any reactions. Your dog does not have to meet any other dogs in public. If someone asks if your dog can meet theirs and you prefer not to, just tell them, "Thanks, but not today." You don't have to explain or defend yourself or your dog.

If someone lets his dog come rushing up to your dog, or a loose dog comes up, be proactive to protect your dog from having to react or deal with that dog. If you take that opportunity to step in front of your dog, blocking the other dog and keeping your dog behind you, your dog is much less likely to become combative or confrontational. You might politely ask the owner to call their dog. If the dog is loose, in a stern voice say, "DOG, COME!" or toss treats away from him so when he goes to sniff or eat them, you can go the other way.

You might want to carry a pop-up umbrella, so when you push the button, it becomes HUGE in front of you. Most dogs will back away. Be sure to teach your dog to be okay with the umbrella when it is open. Get him used to it opening so he is not stressed when you use it. Some people carry pepper spray but Animal Control Officers say it is definitely a last resort and too often people end up spraying themselves or their own dogs.

Eye Contact

We start with food and treats. Also work on eye contact. We recommend not using cues at first with the eye contact. Some dogs are great at making and holding eye contact with us, but many dogs are resistant or shy. For dogs, in dog language, staring into someone's eyes is rude and confrontational, so they may start by tiny glances, or sliding their eyes back and forth, making direct eye contact tricky to catch and reward. As your timing gets better, clicker training works great for this. Start to wait a bit longer each time before you click, if you are clicking, praise and reward.

You can build up eye contact, then start to proof it by moving around the room, turning a bit away from the dog and letting him learn to "seek" eye contact with you. If your dog is looking at your face, he is not looking at another dog or human, and two things have happened. The scary thing has disappeared out of sight because he is looking at your eyes, and you have given him a specific rewardable job to do that makes reacting at anything else incompatible.

This is something to practice several times every day, using food, treats, and play time, anything you can use as a reward. You can put a cue on it. Some people use the dog's name, so when he hears his name, he knows to look into your eyes. Some people use a different cue, such as "watch," "look," or "eye." You can also use the word "here," which means you want the dog to check in, make eye contact, and wait for further instructions.

Once you have the eye contact game going well in the house, take it on the road. Watch your dog closely to be able to reward him when he is checking in with you. Praise and reward his checking-in behavior. The more he looks at you, the less he worries about the environment.

Make it easy at first. Use really good treats, and practice a lot without any distractions. Enlist a friend (for dogs afraid of people) or a friend with a dog (for dogs reactive to other dogs) to help. They should be standing at a far enough distance for your dog to look at but not be alarmed at or reacting to. We do want him to look at his environment, so when he glances at the person or person/dog team, use your cue word and when he looks back at you, reward. We don't reward the look at the scary thing; we reward the look back, when he checks in with you. Gradually have your friend move closer, always working only to the point your dog starts to stress. Watch for longer stares, stiffening body language, muscles stiff, maybe hackles coming up. Stop after one last successful check-in and work more on it later.

If you have a reactive dog, whether he is worried about people, dogs, or anything else in the environment, this exercise can help change his concerns. Too many times we think the dog should be okay, and we leave him to walk out in front of us on walks, making his own decisions about what is scary or concerning. If we start making those decisions, taking that huge responsibility away from him, he will be calmer, more attentive to you, and you can both enjoy your outings.

As always, seek professional help if you are having trouble.

Aggressive Behavior Reactions to Dogs or People Continued

Head Collar, Leash and Harness

Equipment such as the Gentle Leader Headcollar® can be used for walks (see page 130). Please read and review the information included with the GL. There are other similar head collars on the market. When working with a dog with distraction problems, we use the head collar a bit differently than when he pulls ahead. Always keep the leash short (but not tight), so the dog stays by your side instead of walking a few feet in front of you. We recommend a short leash on the GL and a regular leash on the dog's collar or harness. There are times on your walk (for potty times or sniffing to relax or enjoyment) you want your dog to be able to have a little longer lead. Use the longer leash on your dog's collar or harness to let him go sniff or do his job.

The collar he wears should be a flat Martingale (limited slip) or buckle collar he can't back out of since it won't slide easily over his head.

If you are using a harness, be sure it is one he can't get feet tangled in, or get out of easily. Some harnesses clip on the dog's chest, some clip on the dog's back or shoulders. Use one that fits, doesn't chafe or rub his "armpits" and is comfortable.

Body Wrap

Working with a reactive dog is another time we recommend using a body wrap or Thundershirt™ or Anxiety Wrap™. Anything we can do to help keep your dog calm is a good addition. It may seem that there is a ton of gear to use on your dog, and for a while, we might benefit from using it all. As your training progresses, your dog becomes calmer on walks, and you can start to eliminate some things to see how it goes. You can always add equipment back in if you feel you need it, or you are going somewhere new and you or your dog might have a concern.

Question: "I have to walk my dog and we haven't gotten the training to the point he will look back at me. He will do a big lunge/bark reaction when he sees another dog, but I need to walk him for exercise and potty times. What do I do?"

Answer: Make every effort to avoid putting your dog in a position to have a blow up. Take really good treats with you, be prepared to change direction or even reverse your direction if possible. Go at times when others might not be as likely to be out and about. Before you leave the house, practice the eye contact exercise a few times as a warm up and a reminder to your dog. If you get surprised by meeting a dog, as calmly and quickly as you can, turn away and leave the area.

Question: "What if my dog won't take treats outdoors?"

Answer: If you are in any situation where your dog won't take treats he has liked in the past it is a signal to you that he is stressed. It can also be he is just too interested in the environment to be interested in your treats. What is yummy and interesting indoors where there aren't many distractions can become less interesting outdoors with all the smells, sights and sounds the world can offer.

- Try using better treats.

- Another idea is to actually change your reward from treats to an environmental reward. So if you are asking your dog to walk nicely on a leash but his interest is getting to the next tree to sniff or mark, use that sniffing opportunity as a reward for a few steps of walking without pulling.

Some happy endings
from the Animal Rescue League of Iowa

Echo

I believe I got her in 2004 and I was told she was a stray. When I first tested her she had good retrieval drive but would stop to smell other dog smells but because the area was used by all the dogs I decided to give it a shot anyway. After further testing found her to be one of the best dogs that I have tested. Her biggest success was she alerted to an RV that had been stopped on interstate 80 and there was 365 pounds of cocaine found hidden in a compartment on the RV. To this date this is the largest cocaine seizure in the state of Iowa and she was awarded National case of the year for her work. To date she has found over 24 million dollars in illegal drugs. She was also inducted into the Iowa animal Hall of fame.

DG

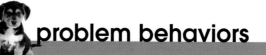

Aggressive Behavior Reactions to Dogs or People *Continued*

Dogs Who Are Afraid of People

Question: "My dog, Jack, usually loves my dad. The other day my dad came over and Jack wouldn't go near him. The only difference is my dad was wearing a hat. What can I do so Jack isn't afraid?"

Answer: Some dogs show specific fears of people, such as people wearing hats. It can be to the point where the same person can approach the dog not wearing a hat and the dog will be friendly. We begin to modify this behavior with the owner showing a hat to the dog. Reward the dog for exploring the hat, then another hat, and another until several hats have been examined, rewarded and the dog has lost his anxiety with them.

Next the owner takes a hat and wears it with the dog, praising and rewarding the dog when he is accepting the hat on the owner. Now that the owner is okay, we move on to other familiar people who are now wearing hats. Gradually the dog will become accepting and know hats are not a problem and can actually be the cause of much rewarding by the owner.

Be careful not to rush this training, or you might make the dog even more concerned about hats. There is a technique called flooding, where the subject is over exposed to the object it fears.

If we "flood" a dog with a scary item, such as putting him in a room with twenty people wearing hats, you could easily cause damage to your dog's emotional well-being. By using desensitization, pairing the appearance of the hat with treats (classical conditioning), we can teach the dog at his own pace to accept or even enjoy people in hats.

Targeting

Another technique used is called targeting. We teach the dog to target something simple. We usually start by letting the dog sniff your open palm (made a bit more interesting by recently holding treats), click and reward, or just reward, for the touch.

This is a great behavior to teach and especially useful for fearful dogs. If the dog is fearful enough he can't touch the palm of your hand, you can try a plastic lid or even a feather. Use anything that does not scare the dog. Whatever you use, help make it interesting with a tiny bit of peanut butter, cream cheese, or other treat applied to it. After a few successful touches, take the treat out of the program except as a reward for touching the target.

Like our other training, do not put a cue with it until your dog is successful and likely to perform the task at least eighty percent of the time. It is an easy behavior to practice several times a day, but quit while the dog is successful. Targeting can be useful in further training, even obedience, agility and trick training, so take a little time and get your dog comfortable with this exercise.

Aggressive Behavior Reactions to Dogs or People *Continued*

The fun part of using this with fearful dogs is it gives them a job to perform for you. After your dog is proficient targeting your hand, repeat the training with someone else the dog is comfortable with. Once he succeeds there, keep moving on to people with whom he is less accustomed or comfortable.

We always want the dog to perform the trick and be rewarded by the owner. Do not ask strangers to feed your fearful dog treats. It won't be effective. Even if your dog musters up the courage to go snatch the treats, he is still frightened and won't have learned anything. Using a target, we can actually encourage the dog to "pretend" to be brave, doing a job you have asked for and rewarding him for that job.

Dog Tales

Good Manners

One of our instructors, Nancy, has a neighbor, Sandy, who has adopted an under-socialized rescue dog, Kira. Kira is terrified of her husband, Joe, and teenage sons. She responds well to a visit in her yard by Nancy's dog, Rio, when the males aren't around.

Nancy took her dog, Rio, to visit Kira, with Sandy's husband Joe and son Tim involved. Nancy gave her dog's leash and treats to Joe. Kira watched the interaction, and the whole group went for a walk. Kira was still a bit skittish, but didn't try to bolt as usual. The next night another dog came to visit, and husband Joe held that dog in his lap. Little successes seemed to help matters.

It is interesting that Kira isn't bothered by noises, but only by male figures.

Nancy has encouraged her neighbor to sign up for the Good Manners class Nancy teaches at the Animal Rescue League to work on getting Kira comfortable around other dogs and people.

Progress on cases like this one can be slow, and family members can get frustrated when the family dog "doesn't like them." It is important to prevent any accidental punishments, such as when Kira could be surprised when a man in the family comes around the corner, or he scolds her for an accident. Rehabilitation of a dog with this level of fear can take months. There are anti-anxiety medications that can be helpful. It is encouraging that other dogs seem to make her more comfortable, especially when she can watch another dog get treats for interaction with people.

Nancy says: What do you think? I am considering having Sandy bring Kira the first night, just to get her used to the building, before all the other dogs show up.

Paula says: How about bringing Kira to the classroom before class along with her friend Rio? A visit to the classroom could help give her a good comfort level.

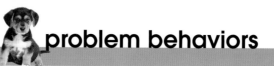
Aggressive Behavior Reactions to Dogs or People *Continued*

Dog Aggression

Q Caller: *Our dog Olive is a 2-1/2-year-old spayed female that is aggressive toward other dogs. Our friends found her as a stray when she was six months old. They took her to the ARL, but the ARL couldn't guarantee she would not be euthanized so our friends asked us to take her. We thought she would outgrow her aggressive personality, but she hasn't. She is fine in our family and with most people, but she is terribly aggressive with other dogs. She's a 45-pound mix, and it appears she has some German Shepherd in her. She has not spent much time with other dogs, and when I took her to the dog park yesterday, she went snarling after almost every dog.*

A Paula says: *I absolutely recommend Olive should not go back to the dog park, possibly ever. Putting her in a busy dog park and expecting her to become socialized is unrealistic. Many dogs are not comfortable at dog parks. If you can find another safe, dog-free place for her to run, that would be better.*

If she is afraid of dogs and has to decide on her own whether to interact, she is very stressed, and is using behavior that makes her look aggressive. You can start helping her by making decisions for her. She can be confident you won't let the scary dogs attack her, and she can be calmer around them. We can teach her to be calm and rely on us to keep her safe around dogs.

Also, I recommend a book called Click to Calm by Emma Parsons. She does a wonderful job of helping her dog become better with other dogs.

Targeting with Dogs Who Are Afraid of Dogs

You can also use targeting with dogs who are afraid of other dogs. With the trainer's social dog, ask the trainer to keep her dog busy with treats while you ask your dog to "target" the other dog's tail. A simple sniff is rewardable. Make it quick by rewarding your dog within one or two seconds. Gradually, many dogs build up confidence enough to be able to do a mutual sniff with the other dog. Always be the one to ask your dog to go sniff or target and then end the exercise with your reward.

Moving away from the other dog is rewarding for a fearful dog, too, so after one or more successful targets to the social dog, give your fearful dog a reward by calling him away. Be very careful not to tighten the leash or drag your dog away from the other dog. Always use a light happy tone of voice and call your dog using whistles, squeaky noises, or patting your leg to encourage him to come back to you. Do not let him stay and explore the other dog, or be rude or pushy. Keep control of the exercise, so your dog understands his role.

With some practice, you could also teach your dog to target his own leash when he sees another dog. This turns your dog's head, which is a calming signal to the dog approaching. Often, if one dog turns his head the other will, too, and they have successfully communicated to each other that there is no threat.

Muzzles

We recommend teaching your dog to comfortably wear a muzzle. There may be a time, such as at your veterinarian's, where your dog is stressed by the procedure, fearful in the environment and needs to wear a muzzle so the staff can do what they must. If your dog hasn't been conditioned to accept a muzzle, you can be sure that if the staff rushes to put the muzzle on when your dog is scared, they will get it done the first time, but the dog will remember and the next time there will be a struggle.

Condition your dog at home to accept a muzzle. There may be times, for example at your veterinarian's office, where he may need to wear one for a procedure.

If you work at home with a muzzle that fits the dog comfortably and desensitizes the dog so he wears the muzzle without stress or fear, then using the muzzle for the next clinic visit will help everyone's adrenaline level to remain normal. Your dog will be calmer because everyone around him is calmer and even if procedures need to be done that might be painful, he can handle it better because there is no struggle.

We recommend buying a basket muzzle that will allow the dog to drink, pant, and eat treats through the wire or leather mesh. Some muzzles are too dangerous for use, because they keep the dog's mouth closed tight and dogs can easily overheat.

Practice many times at home with the muzzle, feeding amazing treats, praising the dog for allowing it to be put on and while it stays on. Teach your dog to offer to put his face in the muzzle by luring him into it with good treats. Just like any other piece of equipment for your dog, he will do best with gentle and positive rewards during the training.

appendix

Topics:

Classes We Offer

Puppy Kindergarten

Top Ten Reasons to Bring Your Puppy
To Puppy Kindergarten Classes:

10. **Poop Happens.** The "old wives' tales" about dogs trying to punish you for leaving them or exacting revenge because they didn't get a treat just aren't true. If your puppy potties in your house, it is because you were not watching her closely enough, she isn't being fed on a schedule, she is being fed too much food or she doesn't understand to potty outdoors. She hasn't learned that if she comes to you with "that look" in her eye, you will take her out to her spot to go. Get your questions answered by an experienced instructor instead of the neighbor, friend, or relative who may not have all the details or experience to actually help solve your problems.

9. **Those sharp puppy teeth.** We call puppy classes "group therapy" for puppy owners. Every owner has problems and frustrations and wants answers. As they ask questions and get information from the instructors or handouts, they may actually be assured that they don't have the worst puppy in the class.

   We commonly hear, "My puppy looks like she is playing, but she is sure having a great time chomping on my hands and chasing my feet.", "Why are her teeth so sharp?", "When will she get over this horrible behavior?", "Do all puppies do this, because my last dog didn't."

   In the course of a dog's life, we often forget those first few months of teething, chewing, housetraining, and destruction, because we had so many good years with our beloved dog. After he is gone, and we decide to bring in a new puppy, we are starting over. Maybe your last dog was the perfect puppy, but we suspect some of the details have been lost in time and this puppy is about the same. You may need some new ideas for relief from those sharp puppy teeth.

8. **Food: puppy food vs. people food.** Dogs need well-balanced, nutritional foods. Many veterinarians warn owners about feeding dogs from the table. The goal is a balanced nutrition. Look for meat sources: meat or meat meal, in the first three ingredients on the package. If the first three ingredients are grains, the food will be quite high in fiber, and the dog will need more food to get the nutrition he needs. What goes in must come out, so if the pup is eating a lot of food, chances are good she will need to poop a lot. When we have owners call about housetraining frustrations, the food volume, type, and schedule are usually helpful in solving the problems. We have found that if you want to start a fight with your dog friends, discussing dog food and what is good and right to feed is high on the list. Everyone has an opinion, and we suggest that you work with someone experienced in nutrition if you are having problems. If you do want to feed table scraps or cooked or a raw diet to your dog, you will want to do some research. Many people feed their dogs successfully with "people" food, but the recipes and balance need to be adapted for a dog's digestion, which is different than a human's.

7. **Sleep.** We all want to get a good night's sleep. New puppies in the house can certainly cause some problems. They cry, whine, howl, and need to go outdoors during the night. Maybe a change in the location of their bed or crate can help.

6. **Crate training: cruel or a gift from heaven?** There is much written about crate training. No doubt it can be cruel if used inappropriately. Keeping a puppy in a crate all day and night seems ridiculous. Learn how to have the puppy out of the crate more without losing the benefit of helping with housetraining and destructive behavior?

5. **Leash.** If you have ever put a leash on a puppy for the first time and watched him try to get away or out of the collar, you will want to know how to help get him accustomed without all the drama. Attending a class can really help.

4. **Puppy play time, or toys, toys, toys.** People getting a new puppy may be tempted to go buy every toy in the store. That is not necessary or even advised. Basic toys will be useful, last, and be well worth the initial investment.

3. **When do puppies learn best?** Studies done years ago first showed the dog world that puppies are brilliant, even when they are tiny. Waiting until a dog was six months old was traditional, and perhaps based on the idea that when using harsh corrections, tiny puppies couldn't be taught. Now that we don't use those methods, we encourage owners to bring puppies to classes as soon as they have had their first vaccination, as early as eight weeks. While puppies attending classes this young may be controversial in some circles, they are certainly learning, and can be taught many amazing things. Many of our foster puppies have started to learn to sleep in crates, sit

and lay down for treats, walk nicely on leash, and potty outside before they are old enough for adoption. One of my own dogs that started out as a foster, learned that "sit opens the door" to go outside to potty when she was four weeks old. She learned to mimic her mother, but she quickly learned to offer the behavior herself.

2. **Meet the cat!** There is so much more to the average household than just the puppy. Often other pets, visitors, and small children can cause fear or concern to the new puppy. Acting calmly and very matter-of-factly when a puppy shows fear is important. We want to identify his concerns, but not coddle him. Instead, pair rewards with the presence of the cat, if the cat scares him. Reward him for ignoring the bird in the cage or the hamster on the wheel. The puppy can learn to watch without interacting, sniff without chomping, and play appropriately as we supervise.

1. **Puppies and children.** We have a chapter on introducing children and dogs. If puppies come to live in a family with small children, puppies and children need to be taught appropriate behavior. If puppies come to live in a family with no small children, they need to be exposed to small children often. Gentle handling by children being supervised by adults will help the puppy learn to enjoy being around children, even if he doesn't see them every day.

Check out these additional classes offered at ARL-Iowa:

Good Manners Classes

Activity Classes: Tricks, Agility, Freestyle

Private Sessions

Finding a Class and Instructor

There are several ways to find classes you will enjoy and that will match your needs. Ask friends, relatives, and co-workers who have dogs about classes they have attended with their pets. Your veterinarian may host puppy classes in his clinic. Your local animal shelter may offer classes.

We recommend auditing a class without your dog before signing up for a class. This will give you the opportunity to see how the instructor interacts with the participants and their dogs.

- Is the instructor informative, answering questions, coaching participants through exercises?

- Is the location clean?

- Is it crowded with too many people or dogs? If the instructor is reluctant to let you audit one class, you have to wonder why. We have always encouraged anyone with concerns to audit one of our classes. Hopefully, you would go home excited about training and sign up right away for the next class.

To find classes available in your area, you can also check websites like www.apdt.com. They list members, many of whom are trainers, and some are certified. If you are in a rural or remote area, it can be much more difficult to find a class. You may need to arrange for a trainer to come to your home for instruction. For some situations, a private trainer can be ideal. If your dog has fears of new people or places, or you need to be at home for family matters, having a private trainer come at your convenience may be the way to go.

If you visit a class or talk to a trainer, ask him what tools and techniques they use. If he uses choke, pinch, or prong collars, electronic shock collars or other harsh methods, we suggest you keep searching. You are looking for a trainer who can communicate to you and your pet without using force, loud voices, or harsh methods.

This is not a situation where "something is better than nothing." If the something is harsh training based on punishment, it really can make many behaviors worse. It can ruin your relationship with your dog, and can actually cause your dog to use aggressive behavior because he is afraid.

Dog Adoption Application Questions

When you adopt a dog from a shelter, you likely will be asked a series of questions to help the counselors in placing a pet in your home.

Aside from the basic questions of name, address, and type of home (apartment, house, condominium, or townhouse), these are some of the topics to be covered:

- Have you ever adopted a pet from this shelter before?

- Have you ever been refused adoption of a pet before?

- How many adults live in your household?

- How many children? What are their ages?

- What will be the pet's role—companion, gift, breeder, companion for another pet?

- Who will be responsible for feeding and training the pet?

- If you have pets or have in the past, who is or was your veterinarian?

- Does anyone in your household have allergies? What kinds?

- If you move in the future, what will you do with your pets?

- If a representative from the shelter wanted to stop by to see how your new pet is settling into his new surroundings, when is a convenient time?

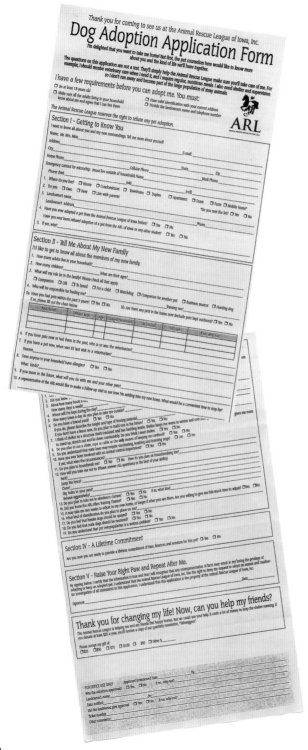

- Do you know that in the first year, regular preventive medicine might cost $150 or more for an adult dog and $200 or more for a puppy?

- Do you know that in the first year, food and pet supplies might cost $100 or more?

- About how many hours per day will your pet be home alone?

- Where will he be kept during the day?

- Do you understand that state laws may require vaccinating, leashing, and licensing dogs?

- Do you have a fenced yard? Do you plan to add a fence?

- Will the dog sleep in your home or in a shelter outside?

- How do you plan to handle housetraining?

- How will you train to avoid barking, jumping fences, chewing, digging holes, and behaving aggressively?

- Do you plan to take your dog to training or obedience classes?

- What kind of identification will you use for your pet?

- How do you feel about spaying and neutering?

Surrender Dog Information

When you surrender your dog to a shelter to be placed in another home, you may be asked some questions.

Honest answers will help the shelter place your dog with people who understand your pet's personality and habits.

- How long have you had this dog?

- Where did you get this dog?

- Why are you relinquishing the dog?

- Is s/he housetrained? When do mistakes happen?

- Does s/he let you know when s/he needs to go outside? How?

- Can s/he be left alone without an accident? For how long?

- Where does s/he sleep?

- Where is the dog during family meals?

- Does your dog chew furniture or other objects?

- Does s/he get into the garbage?

- Is your yard fenced?

- What is s/he afraid of?

- Is s/he good with children under 6? What about 7 and above? Describe his or her behavior around children.

- Is s/he good with other dogs and/or cats?

- Does s/he know any tricks?

- Does s/he enjoy riding in the car?

- Does s/he have any health problems?

- Is s/he current on vaccinations?

- Does s/he adapt well to new situations and people?

- What type of food do you use? How much?

- What are some of the cutest and nicest things about this dog?

A Thank You from the Publisher

Landauer wishes to acknowledge and thank the many people who tirelessly and with great compassion care for the animals surrendered to shelters and especially those who worked to make this book and video happen. Their fondest wish is that there would be no need for animal shelters. Yet, shelters are and will always be needed. Each of us can help—whether adopting, volunteering at, or financially supporting our shelters.

We can spay and neuter.

We can train good behaviors.

We can report abuse.

The animals need each of us.

In particular, Landauer wishes to thank Paula Sunday, dog behavior counselor for Animal Rescue League of Iowa. Drawing on her many years working with thousands of shelter animals and counseling owners on pet behavior issues, Paula took the lead developing ARL of Iowa's *For Love of Dogs* book and video to make sure the advice and guidance are what pets and owners most need to live together successfully. Thank you Paula!

And thank you for lending your rescued-dog Tag to demonstrate trained behaviors.

Landauer also wishes to thank the following people who readily gave time and effort:

- Dr. Dan Campbell, Chief Staff Veterinarian, ARL-Iowa Main Shelter

- Dr. Robert Culver, Veterinarian, Heartland Animal Hospital, Des Moines, Iowa

- Thomas Chaput, Video Photography

- Stephanie Filer, Manager Special Gifts & Partnerships, ARL-Iowa

- Mary McBride who provided the dog park

- Owners whose dogs you see and read about in the rescue stories, photos and videos

- Carol McGarvey, Contributing Editor

- Mick McAuliffe, Operations Manager and Professional Trainer, ARL-Iowa

- Suzanne Tomlinson, Dog Trainer and ARL volunteer and her Border Collies, Bree and Jake

- Robin Abeltins, Brittany Carson-Johnson and Chuck Hall, ARL volunteers

- The ARL Staff and volunteers who assisted us with access and handling of rescue animals for photography

- Special thanks to Tom Colvin, Executive Director, ARL-Iowa and to Carol Griglione, Board Chair, ARL-Iowa, whose vision and dedication, have created the state-of-the-art animal shelter that is Animal Rescue League of Iowa

- Finally, a thank you to the Landauer Staff whose standards-of-excellence and teamwork are second to none

ARL ANIMAL RESCUE LEAGUE OF IOWA, INC.™

For Love of DOGS

SUPPORT YOUR LOCAL SHELTER